Basic Issues in Aesthetics

Basic Issues in Aesthetics

Marcia Muelder Eaton
University of Minnesota

WAVELAND
PRESS, INC.
Prospect Heights, Illinois

For information about this book, write or call:
Waveland Press, Inc.
P.O. Box 400
Prospect Heights, Illinois 60070
(847) 634-0081

To Dennis

Contents

C H A P T E R 3

Viewer-Centered Aesthetic Issues 34

C H A P T E R 4

Art and Language 53

| C   H   A   P   T   E   R   7 |

Aesthetic Value   *125*

Preface

The purpose of this book is to introduce readers to the branch of contemporary philosophy that deals with the nature and value of aesthetic objects and experiences. The aesthetic is an important part of human experience. Our responses to music or mountains are not merely leisure time activities that improve the quality of life; they give meaning to life. Reflecting upon art and the aesthetic requires and generates reflection upon the world and human experience generally.

Introducing students to philosophy is not easy. Even individuals who are not bothered by the fact that there appear to be no "right answers" to the questions philosophers raise are often frustrated because they seem to know less at the end of a course than they thought they knew at the outset. There are additional problems with philosophical aesthetics, for it attracts people from very different areas of interest. Thus one is limited in the assumptions that can be made about background or shared experiences upon which to build. Instructors must challenge and motivate both theorists (philosophy students) who often know little about art and practitioners (art historians, musicians, actors, and so on) who usually know very little about philosophy. Bringing this mixed audience to a point where they can share their special insights with one another is a difficult assignment. I have written this book with the hope that this task will be made easier.

I have tried to write clearly so that the quite sophisticated controversies current in contemporary analytical aesthetic circles are accessible to novices. I have attempted to explain connections between problems in aesthetics and those in other branches of philosophy—particularly epistemology, metaphysics, philosophy of language, and ethics. I have also tried to invite students to bring their own experiences to philosophy and to take philosophy back with them to their experience. I have used examples to which almost everyone should be able to relate, and have included pictures that can focus discussions. While sensitive to the fact that there are no succinct "right answers" that can be discovered even with hard work, I have tried to show that not all answers or views are equal.

The text is organized around components of an aesthetic situation: objects, artists, audience, critics, and social context. Any introduction will cover many expected topics. In this case these include:

the role of objects, makers, and audiences
the nature of interpretation, criticism, and aesthetic response
the languages and contexts of art
the nature of aesthetic value

But I have also included some topics and features that may be unexpected:

discussion of non-analytic aesthetic positions (e.g., structuralism, deconstruction)
practical applications of aesthetics (e.g., environmental aesthetics and aesthetic issues in public policy decisions)
visual material that provides focus for discussion in the text and for classroom discussions

Every teacher—particularly one whose own research is in the area—has his or her own idea about what should be covered in an introduction. Several reviewers made insightful and helpful suggestions about additions and deletions. I have benefited from them, but have not been able to follow all advice. An author who tries to be everything to everyone can in the end only create something boring, bland, and faceless. Refusing this, I have risked being infuriating. Their own power in the classroom will give instructors the chance to show their students where I am too hasty or just plain wrong.

Several people have read earlier or later drafts of the whole or part of this volume: Jerry Cedarblom, University of Nebraska; Donald Crawford, University of Wisconsin; Susan Fegan, University of Missouri; Karen Hanson, Indiana University; Robert M. Johnson, Castleton State College; Michael Reed, Eastern Michigan University; Stephanie Ross, University of Missouri; Donald Sherburne, Vanderbilt University; and Judith Tormey, Temple University.

I also owe much to James Sterba, the editor of this series, whose sustained encouragement prodded me to continue through several drafts. My thanks also go to the University of Minnesota for granting me a Bush Fellowship and Sabbatical Leave in 1984–1985, and to the Philosophy Institute at the University of Amsterdam and the Rijksmuseum of the Netherlands for making resources and study space available to me during that year. Ruth Woods of the English Department of the University of Minnesota and Pat Tompkins provided invaluable editorial assistance. My colleagues in the Philosophy Department provided support of various kinds. The mistakes that remain are wholly my responsibility.

Finally, I must thank my husband, Joe, for his continuing support.

*Basic Issues
in Aesthetics*

Defining the Issues: An Overview

Quite lately, my noble friend, when I was condemning as ugly some things in certain compositions, and praising others as beautiful, somebody threw me in confusion by interrogating me in a most offensive manner, rather to this effect: "You, Socrates, pray how do you know what things are beautiful and what are ugly? Come now, can you tell me what beauty is?" In my incompetence I was confounded, and could find no proper answer to give him—so leaving the company, I was filled with anger and reproaches against myself, and promised myself that the first time I met with one of you wise men, I would listen to him and learn, and when I had mastered my lesson thoroughly, I would go back to my questioner and join battle with him again. So you see that you have come at a beautifully appropriate moment, and I ask you to teach me properly what is beauty by itself, answering my question with the utmost precision you can attain: I do not want to be made to look a fool a second time, by another cross-examination.

Socrates, *Greater Hippias* ▮

DEFINING 'BEAUTY', 'ART', AND 'AESTHETIC'

Theories of beauty and art go back at least as far as the ancient Greeks. Socrates was confounded, as we still are today, by questions that most readers have probably asked themselves at one time or another. People often confidently claim that something or someone is beautiful, but are thrown into a quandary when someone asks them to explain what they mean. One friend says that a film is exciting, another complains that she was bored. A song I am moved by is described by someone else as sickeningly sentimental.

How, if at all, can we support our judgments? When we try, sometimes we become even more confused. We point to features of the film or song to prove its worth, only to have those same features used as evidence of its lack of value:

"What a movie—one car chase after another!"

"I know; I was bored to death."

"The lyrics were so romantic!"

"Yes, that's exactly why they were so sentimental."

The worry about how we can know is at the heart of aesthetics just as it is at the heart of other branches of philosophy. Socrates believed that he could justify his condemnations of things as *ugly* and his praising of things as *beautiful* only if he could provide a definition for those terms. In philosophical aesthetics, as in other areas of philosophy, attempts to define key terms have played a central role. So have questions about how we can know that the definitions are correct and how we can tell if an object fits the definition.

When Socrates was asked, "Come now, can you tell me what beauty is?" he was being asked to define 'beauty', and the question is still debated. It is easy to understand why definition has been elusive, for people simply do not agree about what 'beauty' means. Though philosophers have tried for centuries to define this term, no definition has seemed universally acceptable. Ask yourself what you mean when you say a sunset or a car or a dance movement is beautiful. Do you mean the same thing in each case, even though the things described as beautiful are so different from one another? If you believe that something is a car, you can reasonably be confident that others will share your belief. The same degree of confidence does not seem to attend the belief that something is beautiful. It is precisely this lack of agreement that leads to the old saying, "Beauty is in the eye of the beholder." If everyone uses the terms 'beauty' or 'beautiful' differently, no wonder they have escaped precise definition. More than mere disagreement over words is at stake here. Understanding the very nature of aesthetic activity, experience, and judgment demands explaining how communication is possible when key words seem to mean such different things to different people.

Because the experiences we identify as aesthetic are often connected with works of art, aesthetics is sometimes identified as the 'philosophy of art'. But the question "Can you tell me what art is?" is as difficult as the question about the definition of 'beauty'.

Figure 1   Carl Andre, *Stone Field*. 1978, Hartford, Connecticut. Used by permission.

Contemporary art in particular often leaves us at a loss. We do not know how to approach it, let alone evaluate it. In a downtown public park in Hartford, Connecticut, is a group of thirty-six boulders. They were put there under the supervision of the artist Carl Andre. (At least Andre calls himself an artist; we shall ask ourselves in this book whether he is correct.) Andre called his creation *Stone Field*. Although no local money was used to pay Andre, he received $87,000 from the National Endowment for the Arts and the Hartford Foundation for Public Giving. The total expense of materials, shipping, placement, and so on, has been estimated at $12,000.[1] Thus Andre was paid well for his "work."

What are we to make of these rocks? (See Figure 1.) Can we use the terms 'beautiful' or 'ugly' to describe them? Is there one single work of art here of which the individual boulders are parts? Is there an artwork here at all? The frustration felt by Socrates at the foot of the Acropolis in ancient Athens seems even more pronounced as we confront such puzzling objects in our public spaces (and in our museums and concert halls as well).

Socrates was thrown into confusion when he was asked to justify his claim that some things are beautiful and others ugly. The boulders in Hartford caused confusion for different reasons. Andre and the people who commissioned his work called something 'art' that others were unwilling (and remain unwilling) to accept as such. To the latter an arrangement of rocks did not seem to demonstrate genuine *artistic* activity. Some critics have insisted that "little kids could do it"; others say that Andre has ruined the city.[2] Many people have objected to the money spent on it; one person described it as "another slap in the face for the poor and elderly."[3]

Some people, however, report that they love *Stone Field*. And Andre did attempt to defend himself and explain his work. The group of boulders is located next to a graveyard and, like it, uses stones quarried from nearby hills. The artist (if we can at least provisionally call him that) said that he hoped to unite "natural history with the smaller scale of human history."[4] Andre may also, like many contemporary artists, have wanted to make his audience think about the nature of art and artistic activity. If that was his aim, he was surely successful! But does such success entitle Andre to be called an 'artist'?

Just as troublesome as 'beauty' and 'art' is the term 'aesthetic'. What does it mean to say that someone is having an 'aesthetic experience' or is 'responding aesthetically'?

The term 'aesthetic' did not appear until the eighteenth century, although the history of issues that it refers to is as long as that of ethics, logic, metaphysics, and epistemology. The philosopher Alexander Baumgarten coined it in 1750 to refer to a special area of philosophy. Using the Greek word *aisthētikos* meaning "sensory perception," Baumgarten wanted to produce a science of beauty based upon sense perception. The shift of attention from *things* to *perception of things*, from object to subject, signaled by Baumgarten's concentration on sensory experience, indicates that the central position of the question "How can we know when things are beautiful or ugly?" began to be taken over by the question "What happens when people respond aesthetically?"

I attended college at a small, liberal arts college in the Midwest. Each spring there was an Art Festival—a weekend filled with theatrical performances, concerts, and an exhibit of students' artworks. Experts from Chicago, whose credentials showed that they knew a great deal about art, were hired to judge the works and award prizes. The grand prize my senior year went to a young man known by many locally because his father was a doctor. Many of the people attending the exhibit knew his family. The painting—done in dissonant purples and greens— was of a hideously ugly woman with numerous distorted breasts. It was titled *Mother*, and that year the festival happened to fall during Mother's Day weekend.

Philosophical debates are not always coolly objective. The one that took place in my home following my family's visit to the art show nearly ruined our Mother's Day weekend. My mother knew and felt very sorry for the artist's mother. She strongly believed that the Chicago experts should not have awarded the first prize to such an ugly painting. She further believed that the art professors were wrong to allow it to be displayed—particularly with such a title.

My father, a history professor, believed just as strongly that freedom of expression would have been abridged if the picture had not been hung with the artist's chosen title. My younger brother argued that outsiders could not have known that the artist's mother or her friends would be in the audience. My older brother thought it would have been irrelevant even if they had. I agreed, insisting that judgments of aesthetic merit alone counted—that moral considerations were not at issue. We accused each other of various sorts of insensitivity, but the main charge was that my mother was letting her emotions and moral principles get in the way—that she was not responding aesthetically.

Was this a fair charge? After all, my mother did say that the painting was "ugly," and surely this is an aesthetic description. Doesn't using it indicate that one is responding aesthetically? Is it impossible to respond aesthetically and morally at the same time? How, in general, do we know if and when we and others are demonstrating *aesthetic* sensitivity? What counts as aesthetic activity? Is it enough to look at a painting? Or must we study it in a certain way? Does a special emotion, or repression of emotion, always characterize aesthetic experience? If someone creates a beautiful (or ugly) painting, can we be sure that he or she has had an aesthetic experience?

These questions, and others, will be addressed in this book. I shall not provide a history of aesthetics, but shall discuss current problems and some definitions and theories that have been formulated in an attempt to deal with them.

AESTHETIC THEORIES

Questions about definitions of key terms such as 'beauty', 'art', and 'aesthetic' have led philosophers to try to formulate theories to explain these difficult concepts. In this section, I will briefly describe examples of aesthetic theories and consider a philosopher who believes that theories of the aesthetic are impossible.

In contemporary aesthetics, 'art' is more often discussed than 'beauty'. For several centuries art was considered a species of imitation. (Statues were thought to be imitations of human beings, dramas were considered imitations of human actions, and music an imitation of the harmonies of the universe.) Theorists tried to explain art by distinguishing it from other kinds of imitation in terms of the medium in and purpose for which it was produced. For example, Aristotle defined *tragedy* as the verbal imitation of an action in which a noble hero suffers pitiful and fearful misfortunes and through which an audience experiences pleasurable catharsis (working out) of pity and fear. Some philosophers still hold imitation theories of art, but through the years such theories have been overshadowed by other theories, many of which will be discussed in later chapters.

Theories of the aesthetic often take the form of presenting necessary and sufficient conditions for asserting that something is an aesthetic object, activity, experience, or situation. A *necessary condition* is a condition that *must* be present in order for something to occur. For example, a necessary condition of being a bachelor is that a man is unmarried. Something is a *sufficient condition* if it is *all* that is required in order for a thing to occur or be present. A temperature of −10° Fahrenheit is sufficient for fresh water to freeze.

Ideally, aesthetic theories will allow one to distinguish the aesthetic from the non-aesthetic by clearly stipulating what conditions or properties all and only those things that are described as 'aesthetic' fulfill or have. Different components of what we might call an "aesthetic situation" provide ways of grouping aesthetic theories according to: (1) the maker (at least when the object of attention is an artifact), (2) the viewer or audience, (3) the object or event, and (4) the circumstances or context in which the object, event, or performance is experienced. Aesthetic theories often concentrate on one of these four elements, or upon ways in which these elements interact, and thus necessary and sufficient conditions are often laid out in such terms.

Aesthetic theories concentrating on the artist explain such key terms as 'beauty', 'art', or 'aesthetic' in terms of things thought to be special about artistic psychology or activity. Such theories would answer the sorts of questions that arose in connection with the *Mother* painting by referring to the artist's role. They might say that what is necessary is a special purpose or intention that the artist has. Thus a definition might propose that something is an aesthetic object if and only if the artist creates with the intention of producing an aesthetic response. Or some theories urge that the artist necessarily possesses creativity or imagination. Another kind of aesthetic theory highlights artistic expression or communication. Theories that center on the artist are the subject of Chapter 2.

Aesthetic theories that concentrate on the viewer emphasize the necessity of a special kind of audience experience. These theorists believe that 'aesthetic' or 'art' or 'beauty' is best understood by examining viewers—by looking, for example, at the various ways in which members of my family reacted to *Mother*. A special response (one in which moral considerations are absent, for example) is often at the center of viewer theories. This response has variously been accounted for in terms of a particular kind of aesthetic experience, such as the exercise of taste or taking of a unique attitude. Other theories of viewers center on a special kind of emotional or mental operation. Viewer theories are the subject of Chapter 3.

Aesthetic theorists who believe that the object is most important try to distinguish aesthetic or artistic objects from non-aesthetic, non-artistic objects, without relying on some special quality of either the creator or the viewer. (Their theories will be discussed in Chapters 4 and 5.) Such theories may insist on a particular property—beauty, for instance. Some theories focus on what are called "formal properties" (sound, color, or shape, for instance) and try to show that in aesthetic situations these are the only aesthetically relevant objects of attention. According to such views, only properties of *Mother* matter, not the artist or viewer's reaction. Some of the most important work in recent philosophic aesthetics has grown out of attempts to explain that a special kind of language is present in aesthetic objects. Works of art are considered symbols that only people familiar with the symbol system can grasp. (Some theorists would argue that the type of reaction my mother displayed shows that she does not know how to "read" a painting.)

Finally, there are theorists who believe that what really matters is whether or not the context in which makers, viewers, and objects appear is ripe for aesthetic reception. Institutional theorists, for example, insist that certain sorts of institutions such as museums or conventions governing performance practices or reviewing procedures are necessary before we can make sense of the aesthetic. In the absence of Chicago experts, for example, *Mother* cannot be a painting, let alone a good painting. Nor without complex social practices could a bunch of rocks become a work entitled *Stone Field*. Other theorists point to historic or economic or social conditions that must exist in order for aesthetic experience to take place.

THE POSSIBILITY OF AESTHETIC THEORIES

Although I have said that in later chapters we shall examine and evaluate various definitions and theories, be aware that some people reject the possibility of defining or theorizing about key aesthetic concepts altogether. Not all contemporary philosophers of aesthetics devote themselves to attempting to state the necessary and sufficient conditions that mark off the aesthetic. Indeed, many philosophers are quite skeptical about the possibility of defining key aesthetic terms such as 'beauty', 'art', or 'aesthetic' or of devising theories that explain what is special or unique about them.

One of the most articulate of these skeptics is Morris Weitz, who gives what many consider a convincing argument for the indefinability of the word 'art'. Agreeing with the philosopher Ludwig Wittgenstein that most basic words in our vocabulary cannot be precisely defined, Weitz believes that 'art' names things that bear at most a loose "family resemblance" to one another. He thinks that conditions necessary and sufficient for its proper use cannot be given. For example, consider the term *game*. Soccer, golf, Trivial Pursuit, Dungeons and Dragons, and I Spy are all games. But try to specify anything that they and only they have in common; it cannot be done. What do Beethoven's Fifth Symphony, Leonardo da Vinci's Mona Lisa, and Shakespeare's *Hamlet* have in common? The vast number of things and actions correctly called 'art' seem to make defining 'art' at least as elusive as defining *game*.

The puzzle has intensified in the twentieth century. We have already looked at the "work of art" commissioned for downtown Hartford. Other unlikely objects and events have been displayed as art. Marcel Duchamp's work displayed in a museum and titled *Fountain by R. Mutt* is an ordinary urinal. John Cage has asked us to "listen" to "4 Minutes and 33 Seconds of Silence." Some contemporary poetry anthologies display blank pages as "poems." There are films lasting several minutes that show nothing but an empty hallway and dances in which crowds of people just walk back and forth across the stage. There seems to be no property or set of properties that all of these share with each other or with the "standard" works of art referred to in the preceding paragraph.

Weitz believes that the creative nature of art demands indefinability: "The very expansive, adventurous character of art, its ever-present changes and novel creations, make it logically impossible to insure any set of defining properties."[5] He distinguishes between "closed" and "open" concepts: *closed concepts* are concepts that lend themselves to definitions stating necessary and sufficient conditions; *open concepts* are those that do not lend themselves to such definition. 'Urinal' or 'fountain' may be closed; 'art' is open, he believes. If a philosopher says what 'art' is, the next day an artist will create a counterexample—and would we really have it otherwise?

Some philosophers believe that we can have it both ways, that is, that we can say what art is without denying or precluding its creativity. The philosopher Maurice Mandelbaum argues that Wittgenstein, and subsequently Weitz, failed to notice that family resemblance is a twofold relationship.[6] In addition to physical features that members of the same family may or may not share (a broad jaw, for instance), family resemblance depends upon common ancestry. He suggests that there may be something analogous to this with respect to games and art. There may not be *manifest properties*—features that are directly perceivable, like a broad jaw or a goalpost or rhyming words—but there may be some property that cannot be directly perceived like a causal history of a special sort, or a distinctive purpose, that enables us to distinguish art from everything else. If you look only at my mother and me and have no knowledge about our causal relationship, you will not be able to tell whether we are related. Similarly, if you look only at an object, you may not be able to see how it came into being or what its purpose is, and thus you may not be able to say if it is art or not.

Mandelbaum thinks that because of Wittgenstein's emphasis on "directly exhibited resemblances" and his failure to "consider other possible similarities," he failed to "provide an adequate clue as to what—in some cases at least—governs our use of common names."[7] The inclusion of photography as art, for example, has been tied to the fact that it "arises out of the same sorts of interest, and can satisfy the same sorts of interest, and our criticism of it employs the same sorts of standards, as is the case with respect to the other arts."[8] These features are not directly exhibited, but once we know about them, we realize that photography has become an art form.

But, Weitz's supporters respond, Mandelbaum's statement implies that we know what these interests and standards are when we do not. Just as there are no directly observable properties that all and only artworks have, so there are no special interests that art and only art serves (such as expressing emotion or providing pleasure) and no uniform, generally accepted set of standards for judging works of art or aesthetic objects. Mandelbaum assumes that we can say what the standards are that operate in recognized art forms, but his critics believe that doing this is as impossible as stating what the manifest properties are that all artworks share.

The frustration that accompanies this apparent discovery *is* manifest, and it is not only directly perceivable in debates between philosophers. If we attend an exhibition of contemporary paintings or a performance of modern music, the audience's confusion is often obvious.

In Paris in May, 1913, the first performance of Igor Stravinksy's ballet *Rite of Spring* was presented at the Théâtre de Champs-Elysees. As the music began to be played, members of the audience shouted their disapproval. The music was considered revolutionary; it seemed to break all rules of melody and rhythm. The dancers had had great difficulty with it from the beginning. The composer himself reported that when he worked with Vaslav Nijinsky, the dancer-choreographer, Nijinsky suggested that he count aloud for the dancers while Stravinsky played the piano and that they would just "see where we come out." The dancers continued to rely on Nijinsky's counting (he stood offstage during the premiere), and as the audience's heckling grew louder, it became harder and harder for the dancers to hear where they were supposed to be. Fighting broke out in the hall between Stravinsky's supporters and opponents, and the music could no longer be heard by anyone. In the end about fifty combatants (some of whom had actually had their clothes torn off) were arrested.[9]

This is only one dramatic instance of a public thrown into confusion. The mushrooming of explanatory aids in museums, lengthy written texts on the walls next to paintings, and cassette players that can be rented at an exhibit (indicating what one should look *for* and often *at* as well) signal that the problem of defining 'art' and 'the aesthetic' is not one encountered solely in departments of philosophy. Philosophic skepticism becomes public skepticism expressed in the statement, "I guess art is whatever anybody says it is," an attitude that is clearly similar to one expressed in its precursor, "Beauty is in the eye of the beholder."

The art-is-what-anybody-says-is-art attitude is articulated in a more sophisticated fashion by some contemporary aestheticians. Others, though sympathetic to it, find it unacceptable in certain respects and prefer a version that restricts the "sayer" to certain authorities or experts. In other words, certain people are qualified to say what art is. In both views, it is not manifest properties of objects that make them art or some unique experience of beholders (see Chapter 5). Rather, something special about the social context in which objects are created or displayed results in their correctly or incorrectly being called 'art'. I shall present my own definition of 'art' later, and I hope it will help us to settle questions like those raised in connection with *Stone Field* or *Mother*. I also hope to show that my definition successfully deals with those who believe that defining 'art' is impossible.

AESTHETIC JUDGMENTS AND POLICIES

Another set of problems is raised in Socrates' speech when he asks how we *know* when things are beautiful. In the history of aesthetics, particularly in our own century, this question has been broadened to include not just *how* but also *whether* we can know if something has aesthetic value or not. Are statements made about works of art or aesthetic objects or expressions (both descriptions and evaluations) the kind of statement that can be *proved* to be true or false? If not, is there any way of justifying aesthetic claims or judgments?

When people describe works of art, to what extent can we trust what they say? Are remarks about songs or plays, for example, as reliable as reports about the weather or baseball games? Consider the following paragraph from the *New York Times* theater section of August 5, 1984:

> *The Happiest Days of Your Life* is an utterly enjoyable post-war farce about boys and girls boarding schools forced to share the same quarters. John Dighton, the author, wrote such classic film comedies as *Kind Hearts and Coronets* and *The Man in the White Suit*. For all its outrageous puns and prim public school sexuality, the trifling *Happiest Days* remains endearing in its nostalgia-suffused Clifford Williams staging; Peggy Mount was born to play the headmistress originated by Margaret Rutherford on stage and film. When the cast leads the audience in a school-anthem singalong at the end, the joy seems more spontaneous than at any other London curtain call.

Frank Rich, who wrote the review of this play in London, makes several claims, and it is illuminating to break some of them down.

1. *Happiest Days* is an enjoyable postwar farce.
    1.1 *Happiest Days* is a postwar play.
    1.2 *Happiest Days* is a farce.
    1.3 *Happiest Days* is enjoyable.

2. John Dighton is the author of *Happiest Days* and of the film classics *Kind Hearts and Coronets* and *The Man in the White Suit*.
    2.1 John Dighton wrote *H*, *K*, and *M*.
    2.2 *M* and *K* are films.
    2.3 *M* and *K* are classics.

3. There are outrageous puns in *Happiest Days*.
    3.1 There are puns in *Happiest Days*.
    3.2 The puns in *Happiest Days* are outrageous.

4. The trifling *Happiest Days* remains endearing in its nostalgia-suffused Clifford Williams staging.

    4.1   Clifford Williams did the staging.

    4.2   *Happiest Days* is nostalgically staged.

    4.3   *Happiest Days* is trifling.

    4.4   *Happiest Days* is endearing.

5. Peggy Mount was born to play the headmistress originated by Margaret Rutherford.

    5.1   Peggy Mount plays the headmistress.

    5.2   Margaret Rutherford was the first to appear in the role of headmistress.

    5.3   Peggy Mount was born to play the role.

I have ordered the substatements in such a way that the initial entrants seem clearly to state facts. Perhaps Rich made a mistake; the play might have been written just before the war, for instance. But nonetheless, this and the other first substatements can easily be verified. As we proceed down the list, it becomes less and less clear that Rich is giving us purely factual information about the play. "Objective" data seem to give way to reports on his "subjective" response. *Objective statements* make claims about objects in the world and their truth or falsity is at least potentially a matter of general agreement. A claim about the author of a play (2.1, for instance) is objective. *Subjective statements* are reports about someone's experience or personal reaction and are often thought to be incapable of general verification. Many people would classify the claim that the play is endearing or that the puns are outrageous as subjective. (Interpreted literally, 5.3 seems obviously false. But figuratively it fits into the subjective category—Rich thought that Mount was very good in the part.)

But if Rich is simply giving us a report of his own idiosyncratic reactions, of what possible interest can his article be to others? How can the activity known as "criticism" be of any help to us? If, as many believe, "The play is endearing" is not a statement of fact that can somehow be proven true or false, then including such statements in newspaper articles should seem superfluous. We might believe that Rich is someone like ourselves and that we are likely to react to plays in much the way he does. Or we might believe that critics in general are more sensitive people whose personal reactions are more trustworthy than our own. But since Rich and most critics are strangers to most of us, neither of these explanations accounts for the interest readers take in how reviewers react. The inclusion of reviews in newspapers must serve some purpose other than reportage of facts.

It is helpful, I think, to compare statements such as "The play is endearing" to statements that most of us believe are clearly instances of simple reports of personal reactions or preferences. "Oysters taste awful" is something I often say when my family gathers for Thanksgiving dinner. But my statement is certainly not of general or public interest. When I say it, I don't expect anyone to ask me for my reasons, any more than I would accuse my husband of being irrational for thinking that oysters, even raw ones, are wonderful. Herein lies an important difference between pure preference statements (if we may call them that without attaching too much weight to "pure") and critical statements. We do expect critics to be able to give reasons in support of their evaluations. Is this an irrational expectation? Or is there something significantly different about statements of aesthetic preference, so that reasons play a role but not one of verification? I shall discuss these questions in Chapter 6 and shall argue that aesthetic judgments can be viewed as claims that can be rationally supported or justified.

Philosophers have often compared and contrasted aesthetic and moral judgments. (I will discuss some of these philosophers in Chapter 7.) In Plato's dialogue *The Republic*, Socrates urges the deportation of all artists from the utopia he and other characters propose on the ground that they distract people from what should be their just goals. Morality does not thrive in an artistic atmosphere, he believed. But others—for example, Leo Tolstoy—have thought that morality is likely to thrive only in a society in which true art (art in which sincere human emotion is communicated) abounds. Still others, particularly in our own century, have insisted that it is a mistake to confuse aesthetic and moral value; the two values are, it is often claimed, utterly distinct.

I have promised that I shall later present my own definition of 'art' and argue for an objective basis for aesthetic evaluation. These proposals will, I hope, provide a means for dealing with what I call "applied aesthetics." In recent years, philosophical ethics has become more and more relevant by addressing contemporary problems in our society both inside and outside the academic classroom. Such applied courses as medical ethics, business ethics, and ethics for engineers are increasingly popular, as are demands for experts in these areas in the world outside of the academy. For a variety of reasons, applied aesthetics has been slower to develop. But there are several practical aesthetic problems that I shall discuss at the end of this book. For example, public money is spent in support of the arts (although the amount decreased in the 1980s). In neighborhoods all over the United States and in many other parts of the world, sculptures suddenly appear and poets can be heard reciting their latest verses. National and local commissions have been established whose purpose is to enrich the aesthetic lives of taxpayers. Yet the way in which funds are distributed for such purposes remains a mystery to the average citizen. Questions of public policy and aesthetic judgments are thus connected.

Aesthetic issues are becoming more intertwined with other public decisions. The Environmental Policy Act of 1969, for example, requires that environmental impact studies not only consider a proposed project's consequences for pollution or other social, safety, or health effects on the population but also that effects on "aesthetic amenities" be studied. How is such a study to be carried out? For our purposes here, a more important question is Can philosophical aesthetics be of any use to the people engaged in such investigations? Questions of philosophic aesthetic's role in public policy will be discussed in the last chapter.

Throughout this book, I shall provide examples to clarify the various problems and positions that are discussed. You as a reader are encouraged to consider examples from your own experience. At the risk of becoming, like Socrates, angry at being confused when unable to give completely satisfying answers, you should ask yourself if you know an artist when you see one, or if you know when you are having an aesthetic experience, or if you know when you are looking at something that is truly a work of art. If you believe that a song has been produced by a machine rather than by a human voice, does that affect your belief about whether it is a work of art? Can you *prove* to a friend that your favorite musical group is good? Aesthetics, like other areas of philosophy, is as much a matter of asking questions as of answering them.

NOTES

1. "Indentations in Space," *New Yorker*, 21 November 1977, p. 51.

2. *New York Times*, 5 September 1977, 21: 1.

3. "Indentations in Space," p. 52.

4. *New York Times*, 2 September 1977, III, 16: 3.

5. Morris Weitz, "The Role of Theory in Aesthetics," *Journal of Aesthetics and Art Criticism* 15 (1956): 32.

6. Maurice Mandelbaum, "Family Resemblances and Generalizations Concerning the Arts," *American Philosophical Quarterly* 2 (1965): 219–28.

7. Ibid., p. 222.

8. Ibid., p. 227.

9. For accounts of this incident, see Robert Siohan, *Stravinsky*, trans. Eric Walter White (London: Calder and Boyars, 1965), pp. 41–46 and Francis Routh, *Stravinsky* (London: J. M. Dent & Sons, 1975), pp. 10–13.

CHAPTER 2

Artist-Centered Aesthetic Issues

> *Suppose . . . that a finely wrought object, one whose texture and proportions are highly pleasing in perception, has been believed to be a product of some primitive people. Then there is discovered evidence that proves it to be an accidental natural product. As an external thing, it is now precisely what it was before. Yet at once it ceases to be a work of art, and becomes a natural "curiosity." It now belongs in a museum of natural history, not in a museum of art.*
>
> John Dewey, *Art as Experience* ▌

Without an artist there is no art, according to Dewey. He believed that if something is a product of nature, it does not belong in an art museum. Even if it is beautiful, it is not art if there is no artist who made it. Dewey believed that art is a product of a creative process—a process involving actions and desires that are necessary if something is to count as a work of art. Thus if those actions and desires are missing, no work of art exists. Was Dewey right about this?

Philosophers have answered this question both affirmatively and negatively. As Dewey did, many have suggested that the intention to create is crucial to the existence of art, but others think this is a mistake. The artistic process has also been explained in terms of a need or desire to express what seems central to the production of art.

CREATING ART

What do we do when, in nature, we come across things like Dewey describes—finely wrought objects whose textures and proportions please our eye? If they are small enough, and if there are no laws against it (sometimes even if there are!), we often pick them up and take them home—seashells and driftwood and rocks and pine cones. We do this precisely because these objects are a pleasure to look at. But do we think that they are works of art? If so, when—before we pick them up, or only after we get them home?

There has been much debate about whether the term 'art' refers to a class of objects that includes seashells and driftwood or any "natural products," as Dewey calls them, or whether art is limited to things that people make—artifacts.

Some people think that in art all that matters is the object itself. A beautiful stone, for example, deserves to be called 'art' no matter how it came into existence, they say. Dewey believes, and I agree with him, that 'art' does not refer to products of nature, but only artifacts. One reason for saying this is suggested by the phrase 'work of art'. There must be a *person who worked* on something before something can be a *work*. A rock may be quite lovely—smooth, delicately colored, gracefully curved—but we say it is a *'work* of nature' only metaphorically. A rock can become a *work* of art only if someone—an artist—is responsible (at least in part) for the ways it looks. Only if someone works on a rock can it become a piece of sculpture. (That the actual work done can be minimal was suggested by the example of *Stone Field* in Chapter 1.)

If we are shown a rock, we may not be able to tell immediately whether it is a work of art or not. As Dewey says, externally a rock and a sculpture may be precisely alike. The only difference—but the important one—is whether a person was responsible for the shape, color, size and other features.

But notice that the fact that a person works upon some natural object does not ensure that the object will become a work of art. It only ensures that it becomes an artifact. All works of art are artifacts, but not all artifacts are works of art.

Suppose you pick up a piece of driftwood while walking along a beach and take it home. You could do several things with it:

Carve it, sand it, paint it peacock blue, and hang it on a wall

Drill two holes and stick candles in it

Use it as a doorstop

Take it to science class and show what happens to wood after it lies on the
beach for awhile

Toss it in a storeroom and forget about it

Only in some cases has a natural object been turned into an artifact that is also a
work of art. Theorists disagree about which conditions are necessary and sufficient for the transformation. Some locate the distinction in the artist's psychology; others concentrate on goals that artists set themselves—such as expressing
feelings or ideas.

Sigmund Freud and many psychologists after him have thought that what
makes artistic activity special is artists' personalities.[1] Poems, paintings, symphonies, and films are the result of a special psychological nature. Freud believed
that artists turn their fantasies and deeply repressed unconscious desires into
public objects that the rest of us enjoy because we share those fantasies and
desires—but lack the technique or personality that allows us to express them
openly. Sexual longings and cravings for power that people are ashamed of—
afraid to admit to others and even to themselves—can be publicly entertained by
reading a novel or watching a movie. Socially unacceptable desires and unfulfilled
fantasies can be harmlessly "worked out" via artworks.

Freud's theories are philosophically as well as psychologically important, for
they imply something about the nature of art. If Freud was right, definitions of
'art' may include reference to the special pychological nature of artists. Freudian
theories have been very influential in interpretation of individual works of art as
well as in general theories of art, but they have also been severely criticized. One
critic, Carl Jung, argued that since all people share certain psychological motives
(we all want sex, power, and love, for example), something else must account for
what is special about art.[2] Furthermore, it simply is not the case, Jung thought,
that all people who make works of art have the same personality-type. At best,
psychological analysis can shed light on individual works. To use our example,
psychological theories may help to explain why you pick up a piece of driftwood
(rather than a seashell) and paint it blue (rather than red) and hang it on your
wall (rather than standing it in the middle of the room). They cannot explain *why*
the result is a work of art or *if* it is.

As Jung did, I believe that we must look to something besides personality-type
to explain the difference between artistic and non-artistic activity. The *creative
process* might be used to make the distinction. One feature that is present in the
first two items on the list of things to do with driftwood and missing in the
others is *originality*. Artists change materials and come up with something new.
They are imaginative and inventive. They do not just tell us what the world is
like—they do not just hold up a mirror to nature, as Plato maintained.[3] They
imagine new worlds and present them to others for their scrutiny.[4] Hence
invention seems central to creativity.

The philosopher John Hospers describes creativity as activity that is clearly distinct from merely following rules—activity that is neither programmed nor programmable: "You do not know when you begin the activity what the end-product will be like."5 Unfortunately, this is neither a necessary nor a sufficient condition of creativity. Some of us do not know what the end product will be even if all we do is strictly adhere to rules—trying, for example, to make a cheesecake by following a recipe or to put up a tent by inserting rod A in loop B and rod C under rod A. On the other hand, some individuals seem to know exactly what the end product should look like from the beginning; they chip away at a piece of wood to get at the shape they seem to "see" there from the outset.6

Some people have objected to the notion that what is most interesting and important about creativity stems from producing or doing something new. Rom Harré believes that creativity involves instead the ability to see that certain already existing things or ways of acting work well. New things appear at random, and the fittest survive, he suggests.7 For instance, creative use of color would not involve *deciding* to use certain color combinations for the first time, but *observing* that they work when one happens upon them. You do not first decide to make a candle-holder and then go out to look for wood; when you see the driftwood, you see that it might work that way—and when you experiment, you believe that it does succeed, and you want to show it to others. Learning to be creative then would be more a matter of learning to pay attention than anything else.8

But if being creative is reduced to paying close attention, it does not seem to give us a way for distinguishing carving from candle-holder making or from giving a lecture on driftwood. And in fact 'creative' and 'creativity' are terms used widely; we do not just come across them in discussions of art and artistic activity. We talk about creativity in science, for example; one can be a creative baseball coach or history teacher as well as a creative composer or dancer. 'Creative' can mean "fictional" in the phrase "creative writing" or "how to serve something besides hamburgers" in the phrase "creative cooking."

Even if being creative is an important—perhaps a necessary—part of artistic activity, explaining what is special about artists or artistic activity is not sufficient. Thus aestheticians have often tried to narrow the field by focusing on other features of artists that they believe must be present if you are to identify a work of *art*. One feature that has been widely discussed in contemporary aesthetics is artistic intentions. What do artists want to do when they create things? What intentions lie behind painting a piece of driftwood peacock blue? And are they missing when the wood is thrown in the storeroom? The answer to this question may give us a way of understanding 'art'.

ARTISTIC INTENTIONS

John Dewey and other intentionalists, as we shall call them, insisted that accidentally occurring objects cannot be art. Purpose or intention is a necessary condition of art. Whether this is true is one of the most controversial debates in aesthetics.

Intentionalists believe that artistic action (and all other human action) can only be understood if we know what is being attempted. Plato remarked that poets, like archers, can only be understood and judged if we know what their "mark" is and whether they have hit it.

Suppose I stand in front of a piece of blue driftwood hanging on your wall and try to make sense of it; I try to decide if it is a work of art or just there to cover a hole in the wallpaper. I can see what is there, but I may not know how I am supposed to react. So I ask you what purpose it was designed to serve. You say, "I wanted to create a work of art that would say something about the way driftwood lying on a beach is related harmoniously to the blue sea and sky." I might reply, "Oh, I *see* now." Several people who failed at first to make sense of the boulders in downtown Hartford later accepted them as art upon learning that the artist intended to use the rocks to communicate something about the connection between natural and human history.

The concept of intention has figured in aesthetics in two important ways. Theorists argue about whether artists' intentions must be referred to if their work is to be understood or evaluated. This point of view will be discussed in Chapter 6, where the topics are interpretation and criticism. In this chapter we are interested in whether intention gives us a way of distinguishing artistic action from other kinds of action. We want to know whether knowing what Carl Andre intended to do when he placed boulders in the town square helps us to identify his production as artwork. Is there some intention that you can claim to have that will allow me to say which of the options on the driftwood list are the results of *artistic* activity? Does the intention to be an artist make you one? Must you intend to express feelings or communicate ideas or create something in order for what you do to be described as artistic?

Intentionalists have answered these questions affirmatively.[9] They believe that before we can say whether something is art or not, before we can say whether something is the work of an artist or not, we must know what the maker intended to do. Anti-intentionalists argue that this is false.[10] They doubt that people in Hartford who do not think *Stone Field* is a work of art will be persuaded to the contrary by a statement of Andre's intentions. They believe that your telling me that you wanted to express the harmony of sky and sea will not make an artwork out of something that is not one already.

One of the arguments against using intentions to distinguish artists from non-artists is that artists intend to do all sorts of things when they act, just as non-artists do. Artists say that they want to honor God, praise nature, win the attention of a lover, make money, express misery, incite patriotic action, describe working conditions in factories. As the composer Robert Schumann said, "People compose for many reasons: to become immortal; because the piano happens to be open; to become a millionaire; because of the praise of friends; because they have looked into a pair of beautiful eyes, or for no reason whatsoever."[11] In short, the whole range of human intentions has been exemplified in and through art.

The intention to create something is not sufficient for the production of a work of art according to anti-intentionalists. Knowing what someone intends is irrelevant. Whether something is an artwork is independent of what someone was trying to do, they insist. Either something succeeds or it does not; either it grabs you or it does not; either it is perceptually pleasing or it is not. Trying does not ensure success. Many Hartford citizens continued to refuse to call Andre's work 'art' even after hearing what he had to say about his intentions. Van Gogh's painting *Pietà* (see Figure 2) either has feeling or it does not. What he said will not give it feeling if it is not there. And what Van Gogh might have told us about his intentions will not make something an artwork if it is not one. Nor must we know his intentions *before* we can tell that it is a work of art. If you succeed in creating an artwork, you will not have to talk about the driftwood. Even if you shout from the storeroom door, "I intend to create a work of art now," throwing driftwood on the woodpile is not artistic activity.

Anti-intentionalists also deny that the presence of certain intentions (such as the intention to create) is necessary. Suppose you merely want to make money, and you think there is a market for blue driftwood. You do not believe that just painting driftwood is really creative or artistic activity (so you cannot intend to create art when you do it). But everyone who sees your finished product is deeply moved and enjoys looking at it. Might we not say that you have created art in spite of yourself—in spite of your intentions?

Intentionalists claim that art cannot be distinguished from non-art unless one knows that someone—an artist—intended to make a work of art. Anti-intentionalists believe that an object stands or falls as art by itself—that reference to intentions is necessary, sufficient, or even helpful. I shall argue in Chapter 5 that intentions are necessary, but not sufficient, for something to be a work of art. One cannot create art just by saying, "I intend that this be a work of art." Conditions existing independently of the artist must also be fulfilled.

| ARTISTIC EXPRESSION

We were brought to a discussion of the relevance of artists' intentions by way of considerations of creativity. One kind of intention that is often picked out as special in the creation of art is the intention to *express* something.

One way in which you might try to justify calling some of the things done with the driftwood 'artistic' is by explaining that painting it blue, instead of giving a lecture about it or tossing it in a storeroom, involves expression—the way you feel about driftwood, or the joy you feel while walking on a beach, or your general attitude toward nature and its role in modern life. Expressing feelings and thoughts is widely viewed as an important part of the artistic experience.

Figure 2 Vincent Van Gogh, *Pieta* (after Delacroix): Vincent Van Gogh Foundation/National Museum Vincent Van Gogh–Amsterdam. Used by permission.

Almost everyone in our culture would readily acknowledge that the painting in Figure 2 is a work of art and that its maker was an artist. Indeed, few artists have captivated the contemporary imagination as much as has Van Gogh. It might be helpful, then, to look at what he said about what he was doing when he created this particular work.

Well, I with my mental disease, I keep thinking of so many other artists suffering mentally, and I tell myself that this does not prevent one from exercising the painter's profession as if nothing were amiss. When I realize that here the attacks tend to take an absurd religious turn, I should almost venture to think that this even *necessitates* a return to the North. Don't talk too much about this to the doctor when you see him—but I do not know if this is not caused by living in old cloisters so many months, both in the Arles hospital and here. In fact, I really must not live in such an atmosphere, one would be better in the street. I am not indifferent, and even when suffering, sometimes religious thoughts bring me great consolation. So this last time during my illness an unfortunate accident happened to me— that lithograph of Delacroix's "Pieta," along with some sheets, fell into some oil and paint and was ruined. I was very distressed—then in the meantime I have been busy painting it, and you will see it someday. I have made a copy of it on a size 5 or 6 canvas; I hope it has feeling.[12]

Van Gogh's report fits with a widely held notion of what is involved in artistic production and, by implication, of what is special about art or the aesthetic. The essential picture is this: A person feels an emotion—usually deeply—and produces an artifact, a collection of words, shapes, movements, or sounds, that he or she believes will express the feeling. An audience looks or listens to those physical manifestations and, at least when the work is successful, responds emotionally. According to such a view, artists are special on two counts: (a) they have strong feelings that they want to communicate, and (b) they are able to embody their feelings in publicly communicable ways. There is a rare combination in them of sensitive personality and technical skill.

Emotion figures centrally in explanations of art that emphasize the role of an artist's feelings in the artistic process. Sometimes emotion has been thought to be the very thing that distinguishes art from non-art.

Irrationality

Plato was bothered by precisely the sort of psychological intensity that makes Van Gogh's life dramatic and exciting. Plato believed that artists always approach their work with a kind of frenzy. In an early dialogue, *Ion*, Socrates cross-examines an actor (a poetry reciter) who has just come from a victorious performance. Socrates, pretending total ignorance, asks Ion to explain the artistic process to him. In the course of his cross-examination, Socrates discovers that instead of proceeding according to rational principles that have universal application, Ion has been successful because he was "inspired"—possessed by forces that he does not understand but that enable him similarly to stir up his audience. Thus the listeners also put aside rationality and give in wholly to their emotions. (One need only think of what goes on at rock concerts to see the behavior that Plato was worried about!)

Plato believed that the best society is one in which rationality is as pervasive as possible. Thus it was clear to him that artists—whose modus operandi is emotional and hence dangerously irrational—have no role in good societies. In the *Republic*, Socrates decided that artists should be exiled on just this gound; painters, rather than performers, come under attack in this dialogue. A painter, in complete contrast from the ideal, rational individual, attends to and leads others to attend to and delight in the world of sensory pleasure, illusory appearance, and uninformed opinion, according to Plato. Instead of looking for the truth that lies behind the physical world, artists content themselves with copying it. If we want a society in which everyone strives for truth, artists and their destructive and distractive activity must be eliminated.

In the history of Western aesthetics, several philosophers have tried to show that Plato was wrong about artists and their role in society, either by showing that artistic activity is rational (as one way of seeking knowledge) or by showing that emotion and its expression is essential for a healthy individual and society. As early as in Aristotle's *Poetics*, we find both sorts of defenses. Aristotle says that art, unlike history, which merely chronicles events, provides a rational way to understand human behavior by demonstrating what people of certain kinds are likely to do in certain circumstances. Thus we learn from art. It also provides us with an emotional outlet, Aristotle said. Tragedy, for example, provides us the opportunity of purging ourselves of negative emotions under controlled conditions. We are less likely to be taken over by our emotions in daily life if we have had the chance to get them out of our systems at the theater, he thought.

Plato and Aristotle set the stage for what would be a continuing debate. With respect to artists, the controversy has centered about whether the production of artworks is primarily emotional or intellectual. Are geniuses born or made? Is the success of an artist due primarily to inspiration or to training? The pendulum has swung back and forth. In some periods, great emphasis has been put on the attempt to discover the *rules* that must be followed in order to produce a fine poem or painting. In other periods, such efforts were considered misguided, for it was believed that art is the result of individual talent and *inspiration*, the nature of which cannot be captured in guidelines or formulas.

The early nineteenth-century Romantic movement came down heavily on the emotional side. The poet William Wordsworth's famous characterization of art as resulting from "the spontaneous overflow of powerful feeling" remains very influential in our culture's view of art and artists.[13] Many people continue to view artistic creation as essentially subjective, irrational, or arational activity.

The novelist Leo Tolstoy distinguished science from art exactly along intellectual/emotional lines.[14] Science, according to him, is the transmission of *thought*, art the transmission of *feeling*. Tolstoy was highly critical of what he called the "counterfeit" art and artists of the Europe of his day, because it looked only to the production of pleasure. It failed to concern itself with the clear and sincere expression of the individual's emotions, and thus it failed to express what Tolstoy thought true art should express: the religious attitudes of an age. He was also suspicious of views of art that saw it as appealing to our rational natures, for he believed that artists are not to be valued for the ideas that they can communicate. Their role is not to make us smarter, but more humane, Tolstoy argued.

We sometimes forget that Wordsworth insisted that in addition to feeling deeply, artists must also be skillful technicians. Their "powerful feelings" must be "recollected in tranquility." One of the weaknesses of the emotional/irrational theory of the artistic process is that it flies in the face of many artists' own descriptions of their activity. Although autobiographical comments such as Van Gogh's are sometimes consistent with the emotional view, many deny that this view is accurate or complete. Mondrian is said to have spent months studying the geometrical arrangements of his paintings. Auden's manuscripts indicate hours spent finding just the right word ("hurled," instead of "tossed," "flung," or "threw," for example). With the sort of dedication and attention to detail that one expects from the scientist or historian, Wendy Kesselman engaged in lengthy research before writing *My Sister in This House*, a play about two maids' murder of their mistresses in France. Although the dramatic picture of artistic production—the kind illustrated by Van Gogh, perhaps—is the one that seems to stick in our culture's popular view of the artist, we must be careful: Emotion is not the same as being overcome with emotion. Doing research or hunting for the right note or proportion is not incompatible with feeling deeply. Van Gogh's distress did not keep him from exercising the care and control required for the production of a skillfully crafted work.

Even philosophers who argue about whether artistic activity is rational or irrational can agree that the expression of feeling or ideas is an important aspect of what artists do. The expressive function of art involves not just artists but the audience as well. Let's now turn to a discussion of expression theories of art: in so doing, we shall be led from artists, the topic of this chapter, to viewers, the topic of the next.

Expression Theories of Art

Tolstoy claimed that when art is successful, artists, in and by *transmitting* feelings, actually make members of their audience more sensitive to the feelings and needs of others.[15] Not all people who take the expression of feeling as central to art agree that it has this uplifting effect. They do agree, however, that art is possible and valuable because it involves human expressiveness.

Van Gogh's statement "I hope it has feeling" is perfectly clear to us all. The wish to express emotion is generally taken to be a natural and common aim of artists. The wide recognition of this as an aim and function of art has motivated expression theories of art.

In discussions of works of art, we frequently hear the following sorts of remarks: "Van Gogh's painting expresses deep religious feeling," "The ballet expresses joy at the coming of spring," or related statements involving emotions such as "The poem is sad" or "The movie was depressing." Because such remarks are so common, their complexity is often concealed. But the complexities quickly become apparent when we examine various theories that attempt to make what these claims mean more precise.

According to Tolstoy, an angry or sad author, when successful, actually makes the reader angry or sad. If your blue driftwood is genuine art, I will feel the way you did when you made it; I will share your feelings about beaches, for example. This is a very strong version of the expression theory of art. Other theories do not involve actual transmission of feeling, but emphasize what the artist feels. Other theories stress the role of the object itself; still others concentrate on the audience. All of these theories have a common core: the reference to emotion or use of what we might call an "emotion vocabulary"—words referring to emotions.

One of the reasons that the expression of emotion has been such an important aesthetic topic is that it has often been used in definitions of 'art'. But even people who do not think that expression is a necessary or sufficient feature of art often grant that it is an important aspect of some artworks. Thus an explanation of the phrase "x expresses human emotion" has received a great deal of attention in philosophy, and several definitions of 'express' have been proposed.

Tolstoy's theory of expression is a very strong version, for it actually combines *two* ways of explaining artistic expression: (a) in terms of the feelings of artists and (b) in terms of the feelings of the audience. Each viewpoint can be used alone to explain expression. We might first say that when we claim that artworks are sad or express joy, we are primarily making a statement about the artist. Thus we could state the theory as follows:

I.   x expresses y if and only if the artist was or felt y when producing x.

(The phrase "if and only if" indicates that what follows are necessary and sufficient conditions for what precedes it.) A work of art would express sadness if and only if the artist was sad when he produced it. In support of this theory is our inclination to think of artists as unusually sensitive people whose talent lies in being able to put feelings into words or sounds or shapes or movements. It is hard to imagine that someone who had not experienced a longing for an irretrievable past could have written, "I only know that summer sang in me a little while that in me sings no more."[16] Our admiration for an artist is often tied to our recognition that "that's just how it feels"—that she has captured the feeling perfectly. How could this happen if the artist had not felt that way or had that experience?

There are, however, strong objections to this formulation of the expression theory of art. For one thing, it contradicts what many artists say. Many specifically deny that they felt happy when they wrote their happiest work, for example. Or it seems inconsistent with what we know about their lives at a particular time.

> In Cologne . . . is [Rembrandt's] *un*official self-portrait. He is laughing and, as so often with Rembrandt, we are dumbfounded. Henkrickje was dead; Titus had married and left him. He was in the worst money trouble of his life, and actually had to break open his daughter Cornelia's moneybox in order to pay for a meal.[17]

Even if we believe that he could not have been happy at the time, we still can believe that the Cologne portrait of Rembrandt expresses happiness. Thus a theory of expression that insists upon a necessary connection between what a work expresses and how its creator felt must be wrong.

We can see this as well from our own behavior. If someone asks you to "express anger," you might respond that you cannot do it because you do not feel angry now. But you might also act as if you were angry—for example, pound your fist on the table, shout curses, and glare. As Alan Tormey and other philosophers have pointed out, 'expresses y' (where 'y' names some emotion) is ambiguous.[18] It may describe how someone actually *feels* or the way a person *behaves*. People can act angrily (as if they were angry) even when they do not feel that way. Or they can feel deeply without acting in ways that show their emotions. A man may hide his anger with a cheerful smile. Someone may pound her fist on the table so that she appears to side with one group rather than another—even when she is really indifferent to the actual outcome of a discussion.

Similarly, an artist can paint a person who glares without glaring himself or herself—or without even feeling like glaring. Isn't it possible to imagine an artist angrily sculpting a cheerful statue, or a writer bravely portraying a cowardly deed? Only some uses of 'express' are inferential; that is, only sometimes can we infer how a person feels from his or her overt behavior. Pounding one's fist on a table is an expression of anger, but we cannot infer from it alone that the pounder is actually angry. It may be true that Mary *expressed* anger without it also being true that Mary was angry. John can express cheerfulness without really being cheerful. The non-inferential sense of 'express' in descriptions of artworks (for instance, "The song expresses joy") can say something about an artwork quite apart from making any claims about the inner states that went into its production.

The second component built into Tolstoy's "transmission" version of the expression theory of art, and the place where some theorists locate expression, is in the audience. Thus:

II.   x expresses y if and only if x causes (evokes or elicits) y in the audience.

A work of art according to this view would express sadness if and only if the audience felt sad. This version of the expression theory is appealing because our emotional responses to artworks (and to aesthetic objects generally) are one of the things that makes the art important to us. People value things that "grab" them; they seem unable to remain indifferent to or unmoved by what they identify as great or powerful works of art.

"The song expresses joy" sometimes describes the way people react to the song. They hear it and they feel good. Even their bodies respond accordingly—they tap their feet, snap their fingers, and generally move about in "upbeat" ways. When people say that Picasso's *Guernica* expresses the horrors of war, they often mean that when they look at it they feel repelled and depressed at what it portrays. A recent study reports that the jarring qualities of rock music prevent listeners from falling asleep, whereas classical music actually seems to induce sleep through its soothing qualities. There are even studies about the responses of animals to works of art; cows are said to produce more milk when soothing music is piped into their barns. Thus a *causal* connection between objects and audience response has been suggested as an explanation for 'express'.

However, objections similar to those discussed in connection with artists can be raised here. An explanation of 'express' in terms of audience response is incomplete. Even if people do actually feel depressed after seeing some movies, movies they think should be called "depressing" do not always make them feel that way. Someone in the company of a new lover may not have his spirits dampened even by so sad a movie as the war tragedy *Gallipoli*. Nonetheless, he may realize that it is quite correct to describe the film as "depressing." Sometimes people are depressed when the movie is not itself depressing—a terrible movie may simply depress one about the state of filmmaking.

Here, too, Tormey's criticisms are apt. Theory II confuses the inferential and non-inferential uses of 'express'. Claims about the expressiveness of an object are only sometimes claims about the viewer's own feelings.

Neither the feelings of the artist nor those of the audience are sufficient to explain expression. Suppose we look instead at the object:

III.   x expresses y if and only if x is y.

An artwork here expresses sadness if and only if it is itself sad. The problem is that the things substituted for 'x'—songs, statues, or books, for example—cannot literally be sad or joyful. *Things* do not actually feel emotions. But perhaps III is to be understood as:

IV.   x expresses y if and only if x describes or depicts someone feeling y.

According to this view, a work expresses sadness if and only if it describes or depicts a person who feels sad. Van Gogh's painting expresses suffering because it depicts someone who feels suffering. The ballet *Appalachian Spring* expresses joy at the coming of spring because it depicts people who feel that way. Many expressive works of art can be described in this way.

However, there are still problems. There can surely be humorous poems about sad people and infuriating depictions of happy, self-satisfied people. So if objects themselves are the locus of expression, it must be because of more than content alone.

One of the most important attempts to explain expression in terms of properties of artworks themselves (rather than in terms of makers or viewers) is that of the philosopher O. K. Bouwsma.[19] He amusingly describes an instance of a work that is expressive without evoking what it expresses. A young girl reads a sad novel, cries, and at the same time eats bonbons. Her behavior would be inconsistent if there were actually a direct and constant causal connection between sad novels and sad readers. (Indeed, it is incredible that normal people would ever read sad novels if such books actually made them feel miserable.)

Thus Bouwsma thinks that expression does not depend upon a causal relationship between a work and the audience but instead locates expression within objects. He does this by answering such questions as these: How do people learn to express feelings when they do not actually feel them? How can adults write about the feelings of children, or women about the feelings of men? How can a singer who is grieving give a joyful rendition of an aria? Bouwsma's answer is that people learn to do these things (and artists learn to express feelings) by learning the characteristics of people who feel the corresponding emotions. Why do we call weeping willows "weeping"? Because their branches droop—they share characteristics with sad people, who also often droop. For the same reason, we use 'sad' to describe some artworks. Sad music, Bouwsma says, tends to be slow, just as sad people tend to move slowly. Happy songs are "upbeat"; they bounce along the way we do when we feel good. A sad singer can give a joyful rendition by imitating actions of people who are joyful. Thus we might say:

V. x expresses y if and only if x has properties of people who feel y.

An artwork expresses sadness according to this view if and only if it has properties like those of sad people.

Obviously artists do exploit connections between features of overt behavior and feelings. They do sometimes associate slowness and sadness and exploit correlations between descending minor scales and pessimism. Red signals anger, blue serenity, and so on. But these are rough correlations at best. They cannot account for different degrees or shades of feeling. Use of a minor key cannot by itself signal a difference between expressing grief and disappointment, for example.

Suzanne Langer accounts for artistic expression in another, but similar, way.[20] She argues that we cannot successfully explain the expressiveness of art merely in terms of associations set up between formal properties—such as colors and shapes—and human feelings. Simple-minded associations ("Slow means sad," or "Major keys means optimism") will not work. Feelings, she says, are *in* the work—not, of course, actual feelings, but *ideas of feelings*. Music, for example, is the tonal analogue of emotive life, she believes. The two have the same "logical form."

But how? What is the special form that allows art to embody feeling? Langer's answer is that, in some ways, art works like a language—but not exactly. (The connection between art and language is the topic of Chapter 4.) Language has *associative symbols*—symbols used arbitrarily to point to things. As with sentences that result from putting together words that express relations of various kinds among the things named, art is also an "articulate form," Langer claims. But its elements are not words, nor are they tied to particular relationships, and hence they are freer. In language, we first must learn a vocabulary, but in art we know what is symbolized immediately, without having first to learn a vocabulary or grammar. Feeling emerges from the form—and we get it directly and immediately, Langer says.

But do people always get it immediately? Sometimes people have trouble identifying the feelings being expressed in art from cultures with which they are unfamiliar. To most Western ears there seems little difference between an Indian morning and evening raga, for instance, and it is hard to know what feelings go with which properties. Langer's view does not account for this.

Among the analyses of 'x expresses y' that we have looked at—those in terms of emotions of the artist or audience or the object's content or properties— another problem is a whole range of uses of 'express' for which these analyses do not seem to work at all. Although one can go from "*The Little Match Girl* expresses sadness" to "*The Little Match Girl* is sad," and vice versa, such a shift is not always possible in statements about what something expresses. "Paulus Potter's painting expresses a love of animals," cannot be construed as "Potter's painting *is* a love of animals." This latter statement makes no sense at all. Even "Potter's painting has properties of people who love animals" does not help. Which properties—detail, color, balance—would inanimate objects require to allow us to recognize that they express love of animals?

Guy Sircello's theory of 'express' is an attempt to deal with expression of such things as love of animals.[21] His theory leads us back to artists. He believes that when we talk about artworks as expressions, we are making claims about *artistic treatment*: the *way* the artist depicts animals, for instance. We must use an *adverb*, not an adjective, to say what we mean. Thus we must say something like, "Paulus Potter painted animals *lovingly*." Now we can point to attention to detail, demonstrated knowledge of the subject matter, sympathetic presentation, and so forth. He supports the following version of a theory of expression:

VI. x expresses y if and only if x treats something in a way that demonstrates y.

Sircello's view is that expressing sadness involves treating something in a way that demonstrates sadness.

This theory stresses artistic treatment, but the criticism that it fits only some uses of 'express' is again apt. Does the line "I only know that summer sang in me a little while that in me sings no more" express sadness because something is treated sadly? Are the words treated sadly? We are now faced with explaining 'treated sadly' and so seem not to have advanced very far.

Expression of Ideas

All six of the expression theories considered in the preceding section dealt with the expression of emotion. There is another way of using 'express' that avoids this emotional analysis. We often describe artworks by saying things like, "That is a clear expression of the idea" and "That is a clear expression of self-delusion." Such comments have led some philosophers of aesthetics to concentrate on the expression of thoughts or ideas. Consider again the blue driftwood. One might have wished to communicate not a feeling about the beach but an idea of it. Perhaps the driftwood expresses not joy felt while on the beach but a conception of the nature of beaches—the relationships among sand, sea, sky, and wood, for example. Perhaps, then, what makes artists special is not their ability to feel but to understand.

This way of thinking has led some people to emphasize artistic conception rather than the actions artists must perform to produce an object. Artists must, of course, embody their ideas in some medium such as words or sounds if people are to be able to experience them. But some theorists—the most important of whom was Benedetto Croce—have thought that what is really crucial for the creation of art is the idea in the artist's mind.[22] Art does not just express feelings; it also expresses ideas of feelings. Since ideas necessarily precede any physical manifestation of them, getting the idea in stone or on paper is *craft*; formulating the idea is real *art*. Anyone can paint driftwood blue and hang it on a wall; the real contribution comes in having the idea to do this in the first place. Expression understood in this way is a *mental*, not a physical, phenomenon.

John Dewey proposed another kind of expression theory of art, one that takes account of the crucial role of the crafted object as well as the contribution made by an artist's feelings and conceptions. Dewey based his theory of art on a theory of experience.[23] *Having an experience* is to be distinguished, he urged, from just being alive. That is, an experience is a coherent unit that relates features present in the complex interactions between a human organism and the chaotic welter of things that act on him or her. Walking on the beach becomes *a walk on the beach* when parts are organized—when there is a clear beginning, middle, and end, for instance—when some structure draws the various events and reactions together. Artists provide us with experiences by producing structured objects or events that bring together various aspects of disjoint perceptions and organize them into coherent wholes.

Experiences, according to Dewey, always begin with "impulsions"—needs or desires. They continue as intentions are formed and obstacles are encountered and surmounted. Expressions are reflective experiences. They are not just actions in which one gives way to impulse—for example, you suddenly kick a piece of driftwood because you are angry with your lover. An expression involves values that go beyond the mere moment at which one acts, and it involves a "development" of what is felt, a "working out to completion." According to Dewey's account, an expression is not a spewing out, but an organization, so the artist must be aware of the meaning of what is being done. This entails purposefulness—a consciousness of action as a means to a particular end. And this in turn necessitates awareness of the *medium*. The emotion, in a sense, is put into or transformed into an object. Thus in art, the *object* is as important as the artist's feelings and ideas. The artist must consciously use sounds or sights to convey meanings. In art, "Expression as personal act and objective result are organically connected," wrote Dewey.[24] Instead of just kicking it, you consciously use the driftwood to communicate and generate experiences.

Dewey was rather critical of Van Gogh's work. He thought that although many of that painter's creations "have an intensity that arouses an answering chord, . . . there is an explosiveness due to absence of assertion of control. In extreme cases of emotion it works to disorder instead of ordering material. Excessive emotion obstructs the necessary elaboration and definition of parts."[25] (Look again at Figure 2; ask yourself if this seems to be a fair criticism of this work.)

Dewey's use of 'expression' is very broad. It includes many things that go beyond what we normally take to be works of art or even aesthetic objects. Even smiles, if they are purposefully used to create a sense of welcome, are artistic expressions in his view.[26] Any of the items on our list of things to do with driftwood might qualify. Thus one might object that his interpretation does not give us an adequate method for distinguishing artistic production from other kinds of human action. It does indicate, however, why artists are a necessary condition for the existence of art.

In this section we have looked at theories of expression that highlight artists, audience, and objects. All have had some appeal but weaknesses, too. I suggest that there may be no general theory of expression, that is, no theory that will explain all of the uses of 'express'. In this term's wide variety of uses, people do sometimes intend it inferentially—to say something about a causal connection between the state of the creator and the object or about their own actual emotional response. At other times it indicates the presence of patterns of features or actions that are referred to by terms that name emotions (such as 'sad' or 'angry') and that are possessed literally or figuratively by inanimate as well as animate objects.

Often we will know whether someone is talking about the work, the artist, or herself. If someone says, "Brahms's *German* Requiem was written just after his mother died and expresses great sadness," something is probably being said about the artist. If, on the other hand, someone who is crying says, "Brahms's *German*

Requiem expresses great sadness," the speaker probably is saying something about himself. "Brahms's *German* Requiem expresses sadness through a slow tempo and minor intervals" says something about the work and may invite no inferences concerning the composer or his own feelings. This statement may be interpreted as one about the idea communicated in the work. Ultimately, the meaning of 'express' will depend upon the context of its utterance.

| SUMMARY

Many contemporary aesthetic issues concern the nature of artistic activity. The creative process is sometimes used to characterize what is special about art. But creativity is not limited to artists, and thus theorists often turn to artistic intentions and expressions in an attempt to explain what is special about artistic production.

Intentionalists and anti-intentionalists debate the necessity of reference to artistic intentions. Intentionalists argue that art can only be understood as a product of conscious, intentional activity. Anti-intentionalists disagree; they believe that intention provides neither a necessary nor sufficient condition for distinguishing art from non-art.

An artist's need or desire to express himself or herself is something people often mention when they discuss artworks. Several explanations of expression of emotions and ideas—some going beyond artists to objects and viewers—have been proposed. We have looked at expression in terms of an artist's own experiences, the experiences communicated to an audience, and the properties of the product created. These theories, however, capture only part of what is meant by the word 'express'.

Creative intentions and the expressive function of art involve ways in which artists hope to affect their audience. We saw that claims about expressiveness can also be claims about feelings evoked when people experience works of art or claims about the works themselves. Thus we are led from issues involving the artistic component of the aesthetic situation to issues surrounding the viewer and the object.

| NOTES

1. See, for example, Sigmund Freud, *Introductory Lectures in Psychoanalysis* (trans. and ed. James Strachey (New York: Liveright, 1977).

2. Carl Jung, *Contributions to Analytical Psychology*, trans. H. G. Baynes and Cary F. Baynes (London: Routledge & Kegan Paul, 1928).

3. Plato, *Republic*, Book 10.

4. See, for example, Ina Lowenberg, "Creativity and Correspondence in Fiction and Metaphor," *Journal of Aesthetics and Art Criticism* 36, no. 3 (1978): 341-50.

5. John Hospers, "Artistic Activity," *Journal of Aesthetics and Art Criticism* 43, no. 3 (1985): 243-55.

6. For a discussion of two theories of creativity—the "propulsion" and "finalistic" views— see Monroe Beardsley, "On the Creation of Art," *Journal of Aesthetics and Art Criticism* 23, no. 3 (1965): 291-304.

7. Rom Harré, "Creativity in Science," in *The Concept of Creativity in Science and Art*, ed. Dennis Dutton and Michael Krausz (The Hague: Martinus Nijhoff, 1981), 19-46.

8. Francis Sparshoot, "Every Horse Has a Mouth," in Dutton and Krausz, *The Concept of Creativity*, pp. 47-73.

9. For examples of the intentionalist position, see E.M.W. Tillyard and C. S. Lewis, *The Personal Heresy* (London: Oxford University Press, 1939); Ananda Coomaraswamy, *Figures of Speech or Figures of Thought* (London: Luzac, 1946); and E. D. Hirsch, *Validity in Interpretation* (New Haven, Conn.: Yale University Press, 1976).

10. For examples of the anti-intentionalist position, see W. K. Wimsatt and Monroe Beardsley, *The Verbal Icon* (Lexington: University of Kentucky Press, 1954); and Isabel Hungerland, "The Concept of Intention in Art Criticism," *Journal of Philosophy* 52 (1955): 733-42.

11. Robert Schumann, *On Music and Musicians* (New York: Pantheon Books, 1946), p. 70.

12. Vincent van Gogh, *Further Letters of Vincent van Gogh to His Brother*, trans. Johana van Gogh (Boston: Houghton-Mifflin, 1930), pp. 380-81.

13. William Wordsworth, *Preface to Lyrical Ballads*, in *Selected Poems of William Wordsworth*, ed. George W. Meyer (New York: Appleton-Century-Crofts, 1950), 1-24. (Originally published 1800.)

14. Leo Tolstoy, *What Is Art?* (London: Oxford University Press, 1938; first published 1898).

15. Ibid.

16. Edna St. Vincent Millay, "What Lips My Lips Have Kissed, and Where, and Why," in *Collected Poems*, ed. Norma Millay (New York: Harper & Row, 1956).

17. Kenneth Clark, *An Introduction to Rembrandt* (New York: Harper & Row, 1978), p. 35.

18. Alan Tormey, *The Concept of Expression* (Princeton, N.J.: Princeton University Press, 1971).

19. O. K. Bouwsma, "The Expression Theory of Art," in *Philosophical Analysis*, ed. Max Black (Ithaca, N.Y.: Cornell University Press, 1950).

20. Suzanne Langer, see especially *Problems of Art* (New York: Scribner's, 1957), pp. 13-26.

21. Guy Sircello, *Mind and Art* (Princeton, N.J.: Princeton University Press, 1972).

22. Benedetto Croce, *Aesthetics as Science of Expression and General Linguistic*, trans. Douglas Ainslie, 2d ed. (London: P. Owen, 1962); for a similar theory, see R. G. Collingwood, *The Principles of Art* (New York: Oxford University Press, 1958).

23. John Dewey, *Art as Experience* (New York: Minton, Balch, 1934), pp. 35-50.

24. Ibid., p. 82.

25. Ibid., p. 70.

26. Ibid., p. 63.

Viewer-Centered Aesthetic Issues

Films . . . tend to weaken the spectator's consciousness. Its withdrawal from the scene may be furthered by the darkness in moviehouses. Darkness automatically reduces our contacts with actuality, depriving us of many environmental data needed for adequate judgments and other mental activities. It lulls the mind. . . . Devotees of film and its opponents alike have compared the medium to a sort of drug and have drawn attention to its stupefying effects. . . . Doping creates dope addicts. It would seem a sound proposition that the cinema has its habituees who frequent it out of an all but physiological urge. They are not prompted by a desire to look at a specific film or to be pleasantly entertained; what they really crave is for once to be released from the grip of consciousness, lose their identity in the dark, and let sink in, with their senses ready to absorb them, the images as they happen to follow each other on the screen.

Siegfried Kracauer, *Theory of Film* |

Siegfried Kracauer believes that something special happens, to people in a darkened movie theater, and he tries to describe and account for this experience.[1] In contemporary aesthetics several important theories deal with the role of participants in what I earlier referred to as an "aesthetic situation." People often claim that there is something special, even unique, about aesthetic experiences—something that sets them apart from other sorts of human experience. The question this chapter addresses is whether there is something unique that can be identified as an aesthetic experience.

One way to approach the issue of aesthetic experience is to imagine trying to accomplish the following task. (Philosophers call this kind of exercise a "thought experiment.") Go into a movie theater and divide the audience into two groups. On the left side of the auditorium, seat all of the people you believe are having an aesthetic experience; on the right side, seat those who are not. (Performing this task will suggest answers to questions about the proper ways to look at and discuss the *Mother* painting mentioned in Chapter 1.) Suppose the film is a tragedy and that you are allowed to watch and interview individual viewers. Some cry openly. One person sobs and says, "It's so sad—I just love it!" Another, dry-eyed and shaking her head, says that all the blubbering turns her off and that "these people have no taste." One man sits so enrapt that he seems unable to hear your questions and does not say anything. Another launches into a lecture on the role of oblique camera angles in contemporary European films. Who goes on the left side?

How might this task be accomplished? Theories of aesthetic experience suggest three different strategies. The decision about where to seat whom could be made by determining whether a person (1) is exercising a special faculty (a faculty that always and only functions when someone has an aesthetic experience), (2) is exercising ordinary faculties but in special ways, or (3) is focusing on special features of an object or event. Let's look more closely at these three special strategies.

SPECIAL FACULTIES

Taste

One of the characters in the preceding scenario accused other members of having "no taste." In the eighteenth century the concept of taste was introduced to explain aesthetic experience, and it remains very influential. In "Of a Standard of Taste," an essay written in 1757, the British philosopher David Hume argued that taste is a human faculty analogous to the senses of sight and hearing and that judgments of taste therefore have the same empirical foundation as do judgments about what we see or hear.[2] It is *true* that grass is green and that the first string of a violin in tune is a G. There are color-blind and tone-deaf people who misperceive these facts—they don't know the color of grass or the pitch of the string.

Nonetheless, people with the proper psychological and physiological machinery are able to perceive and agree about these things. Similarly, Hume thought, competent judges, people in a "sound state of the organism" who have and exercise taste, perceive and know, to use Hume's example, that Milton is a better poet than Ogilvie. The fact that almost no one anymore knows who Ogilvie is seems to support his view. Hume proposed that standards of taste, like color charts, could be produced by studying the assessments of competent judges (people with taste).

In our century, Frank Sibley has used taste to distinguish the aesthetic from the non-aesthetic.[3] Put simply, he believes that we experience things aesthetically when we exercise our taste—given, of course, that we have taste to exercise. This becomes apparent, he says, when we examine the sorts of things people say about works of art and aesthetic objects.

Let us do what Sibley proposes and look at a description of the Van Gogh painting in Chapter 2. (See Figure 2.)

> During his convalescence at Saint-Remy, Vincent was often occupied with religious thoughts. It was at this time that he painted a number of biblical themes; with characteristic sincerity, he did not conceive the religious figures from imagination—for he was no longer a believer, although he admired Christ as the greatest example of self-sacrifice and love. His religious pictures were copied and transposed into color from reproductions or prints of older masters, Delacroix and Rembrandt. In the choice of the subjects, the motive of Van Gogh's religious paintings is evident: the dead Christ in the arms of the Virgin, the Raising of Lazarus, the Good Samaritan—all these represent a suffering figure and intimate a future salvation.
>
> Copying Delacroix's studied composition and figures, Van Gogh translates the lines and colors into his own more awkwardly pathetic and intense language, breaking the silhouettes, multiplying the visible brush-strokes, and accenting the span of yellow and blue. The shadow of the Virgin's clothes is of an absolute dark blue, like his most visionary and tempestuous skies. Christ's shroud, in contrast, is whitish yellow, daringly lined with blue shadows. The same dramatic opposition of yellow and blue divides the sky into two great zones. The pink and green in Christ's flesh are correspondingly repeated in the rocks at the right. The head of Christ, with reddish beard and green shadows, recalls Van Gogh's self-portraits, through the color alone; the features have another form.
>
> In the more jagged and intense movement of the whole,

> in the contrast of broken and sinuous forms, and in the
> wavy lines that meet in a prolonged pointed tip like a leaf—
> as at Christ's left shoulder and the ground—we recognize
> Van Gogh's conversion of Delacroix's resilient curves. But
> this copy also permits us to see the kinship of his painting at
> Saint-Remy with Romantic and Baroque art.[4]

Sibley believes that the remarks in the preceding passage fit into two categories. Some mention properties that can be perceived by anyone who has normal sight and intelligence: that the painting has a religious subject, that there is a span of yellow and blue, that Christ has a beard, that wavy lines meet in a pointed tip like a leaf. Other remarks—for example, that there is a "dramatic opposition of yellow and blue," or "intense movement of the whole," or "resilient curves" and "studied composition"—require more. In order to judge whether these properties are present, one must have special perceptiveness, sensitivity, or powers of discrimination. One must exercise taste. If you have taste, you perceive directly that the curves are resilient. If you have the necessary sensitivity, you do not infer that the composition is studied or dramatic; you just see it. (This is similar to our use of color vision. You do not reason that the carrot in your kitchen is orange—you just see that it is.) Thus Sibley would derive his movie theater seating chart by seeing who in the audience is exercising taste.

Sibley does not give an argument in support of his claim that there is a distinction between ordinary and special perception. Instead he claims that this matches our intuitions. In fact, his intuitions and mine do not match. I think color should appear as an aesthetic property, but according to Sibley anyone with *normal* sight can perceive this.[5] Since *taste* is not required, color cannot be an aesthetic property. But this may just be a quibble over which property terms go on the list of aesthetic terms and which go on the list of non-aesthetic terms. The more critical issue is whether the rationale for the list itself makes sense.

As Hume did, Sibley believes that although aesthetic properties depend upon an exercise of taste, they are nonetheless properties about which judgments are *objective*. We can say definitely that a painting has a patch of yellow because a faculty exists that allows us to perceive it. For the same reasons, we can say that as a matter of *fact* the painting is dramatic. There is what Sibley calls "a convergence of judgment" about which paintings are dramatic just as there is about which patches are yellow. Though the number of people with adequate taste is smaller than the number of people with adequate color vision, agreement among them constitutes the basis from which objective standards can be generated in aesthetic cases as well: Since most people with taste perceive that Milton's poetry is better than Ogilvie's, it is true that Milton is a better poet than Ogilvie.

Certainly some people seem to be more sensitive and discriminating than others; we all know people who notice things about works of art that others miss. Without having it pointed out, we might have overlooked the fact that Van Gogh's sky is divided dramatically into two zones. People read reviews of movies not just to get advice about whether or not to spend their money on them but also because they appreciate special insights of reviewers. Someone who has studied music often seems to hear things that untrained listeners do not hear. Aesthetic experience does seem to require a special perceptiveness.

There are problems, however, with trying to explain the heightened awareness or capacity for aesthetic experience demonstrated by some people in terms of 'taste'. For one thing, it simply isn't a clear concept. Unlike vision, it isn't a "locatable" faculty, and we do not have ways of settling disputes—there is nothing analogous to a color chart to which we can refer. That is, in spite of Hume's confidence that we could discover them, there are no "laws of taste" on which there has been much convergence of judgment.[6]

How could we construct a taste-test to determine which people in the movie theater are having an aesthetic experience? Is there some great movie that could be used? Even if there were, how can we tell if someone who says, "This is good," really likes it or only knows he is supposed to like it? What if someone says, "I know this is supposed to be a great movie, but I think there are serious defects in it." Does this remark indicate lack of taste—or taste that has been fully developed?

The use of 'special sensitivity' is also suspect. It is doubtful that most people who see the ugliness of the steel producing area outside of Chicago or the beauty of a sunset have, or would claim to be exercising, a *special* faculty. There are also political pitfalls here. It has been too easy to equate the class of people who have taste with the elite or power class. "Experts" have all too often turned out to be conservative dogmatists later exposed as blind to the virtues of budding young artists. At the same time, it is easy to say to someone who disagrees with our judgments, "You have no taste," but hard to explain why we cannot be accused of the same thing by that person.

The Viewer's Emotion

In Chapter 2 we looked at expression theories of art. One of the theories explained art's expressiveness in terms of emotion aroused in the audience. Saying that a poem is sad, according to this view, means that the poem makes its readers sad. We saw there that this view has problems. Sometimes people say that a poem is sad even if their own or others' happiness is not affected by it.

Nonetheless, feeling does seem to be an important part of aesthetic experience. Even if all sad poems do not make everyone sad, at least it seems correct to say that some sad poems make some of us sad sometimes. We *feel* something when we look at a beautiful sunset; we are moved by some songs. People frequently say things like "It brought tears to my eyes" or "It gave me goosebumps" when they talk about their aesthetic experiences. Perhaps the people in the theater who are crying are the ones who should be seated on the left (the side reserved for people having an aesthetic experience).

Formalist theorists (who will be discussed in detail in Chapter 5) often maintain that a special way of feeling characterizes people who have genuinely aesthetic experiences of works of art. But they are less interested in describing the emotion or feeling than in describing what it is about objects that gives rise to it. Thus a special viewer emotion is less central than special features of the object in their explanation of the aesthetic. Furthermore, formalist theorists believe that only artworks evoke the response, so theirs is more a theory of the artistic than of the aesthetic. As I pointed out earlier, the class of aesthetic objects and events is broader than the class of artworks. Thus a theory of artworks may not be an adequate theory of aesthetics.

Instead of taste, a special emotion might provide a way of identifying people who are having an aesthetic experience. The trouble is that there seems to be no single aesthetic emotion. We do not have a word to put in place of 'aesthetically' in "I felt (aesthetically) while I watched the movie." Instead it appears that a variety of emotions can be involved—a variety of *ordinary* emotions. If there is no special aesthetic emotion, perhaps there are special ways that the emotions operate in aesthetic experiences or special objects of those emotions. Let us turn to these other strategies for deciding on the correct seating chart for our movie theater.

SPECIAL OPERATIONS
Ordinary and Extraordinary Emotional Responses

If sad movies really made us unhappy, it would be odd for any of us ever to go to see them (unless Kracauer is correct about our "addiction"). In recent years there has been a great deal of discussion of this problem—the problem of negative emotions. Controversy has centered about the question of whether emotional responses in aesthetic situations are *real* or whether emotional faculties are operating in unusual ways. In many ways the emotions seem to be real. People cry with sadness, laugh with glee, shriek in terror. Laughter and cheer are not hard to deal with, for these are things normal people always seek. But why would they ever go out of their way, as they often do, to see a tragedy—spend money, rearrange schedules, travel in bad weather—in order to put themselves in situations that sadden or terrify them?

Aristotle suggested that people attend tragedies because they enjoy the consequences—feelings of psychological well-being that come from a purging of fear and pity.[7] Thus he believed that the fear and pity are *real*. Going to the theater provides us with a socially acceptable means of blowing off steam.

The eighteenth-century British philosopher Edmund Burke wrote that we sometimes find ourselves in situations that would typically be sad or terrible, but when we respond aesthetically we do not actually feel ourselves involved or threatened. When this happens we feel *delight*—thus our fear or sadness is *not real*.[8] When people are significantly distanced from things, delight replaces the unpleasant emotions. We enjoy a fire if it is in an empty building across the street, but not if it is in our house. Art distances for us—that is, it creates a context in which we are removed from our ordinary interests. We know that what we are watching or reading is not real, or does not actually endanger us, so delight replaces fear or pity.

But Burke's theory leaves positive emotions unexplained, and in denying reality to painful emotions like horror and sadness, we run the risk of having to say that our pleasures—joy or exhilaration, for example—are also unreal. If a wartime tragedy like *Gallipoli* or a shocking horror story like *The Birds* does not really make us sad or afraid, does it not follow that a comedy like *Back to the Future* does not make us happy or amused? If "Don't cry, it's just a movie" makes sense, what about "Don't smile, it's just a movie"?

We need an explanation that will be general enough to cover pleasures as well as pains—that is, not explain away pains at the expense of explaining away pleasures. We also need a theory that will accommodate people who claim that when they have aesthetic experiences they do not put their everyday concerns aside; they do not distance themselves. Some aesthetic experiences seem to *depend* upon those concerns, to depend precisely on who we are as individuals. Being a woman or a parent or a soldier or a black or an Australian or an alto seems central to various aesthetic responses. These are *real* roles that involve real feelings. But if aesthetic response involves real emotions, we come around again to having to explain why one would seek pain.

Colin Radford has suggested that emotional experiences of works of art are real enough but that they are "incoherent."[9] People really become sad or terrified, he says, but these are irrational reactions because the participants know that the situations are unreal and that they should thus not feel these ways. This view is consistent with some individuals' reactions. Some people report that they feel foolish crying at a tearjerker—that they are aware that they are being manipulated and yet lose control in spite of themselves. Thus their behavior is incoherent.

But isn't it odd to think that all and only the incoherent people in the theater belong on the aesthetic-experience side? Radford, I think, misunderstands what happens.[10] We really do feel pity for a tragic character such as Anna Karenina and do not feel childish or crazy when we respond as we do—quite the contrary.

Susan Feagin believes that the whole problem can be avoided if we understand our responses to art as *metaresponses*—responses to responses.[11] People do really feel sorrow—real, ordinary sorrow. They seek it out by deliberately putting themselves in the presence of sad artworks because they take pleasure at their ability to respond in ways they think are appropriate. We derive satisfaction from believing that we are sensitive, feeling people. Thus delight is a metaresponse: in this case a responding with delight to the ability to respond with sadness.

Gary Iseminger has suggested that there are two ways to answer the question of whether we feel real emotions when we respond aesthetically to something. One is the integrationist view: sadness contributes to pleasure. (Feagin's is one version of this kind of view.) Iseminger favors the second, the coexistentialist view: sadness exists simultaneously with pleasure, but is overwhelmed by pleasure.[12] If we watch a sad movie, it makes us sad, but we also get pleasure from watching good acting, interesting camera work, or a suspenseful plot. The pleasure more than compensates for the distress, and this explains why we go to tragic or terrifying movies and seek out other distressing artworks.

Each of the ways of answering why we seek out pain describes a range of responses. Sometimes people act irrationally; sometimes they are not really terrified; sometimes there is real, overwhelming sorrow (so much sometimes that people actually avoid certain films or books or operas); sometimes joy outweighs sorrow; sometimes sorrow contributes to joy; and sometimes we are just pleased with ourselves for being such sensitive creatures. None of these explanations provides a *general* account of what goes on, and maybe it is a mistake to look for such an account. One task for aesthetics is to try to distinguish those situations in which we do seem to respond in ordinary, "real" ways from those in which we do not.

My own answer to the problem is that in those cases where negative emotions are really present the responder must be in sufficient *control* of the situation.[13] Just as genuinely fun rides on a roller coaster involve, indeed require, some amount of real fear, positive aesthetic experiences that include an element of real fear must be such that the experiencers believe that the overall situation is under control. If the fear or sadness is so intense that the viewer is no longer able to concentrate on the colors, sounds, or artistic technique, for example, then the experience ceases to be aesthetic. Later in the chapter, we will look at the issue of correct focus in an aesthetic experience.

Another way of approaching the problem rests on a general account of aesthetic value. The way we feel certainly plays a role in aesthetic experience and is part of what we value in those experiences. In Chapter 7 I shall discuss aesthetic value and provide some clues for solving the problem of negative emotions.

Special Attitudes

Frequently, aesthetic experience has been analyzed in terms of the special *attitudes* that viewers have toward an object or an event. When these attitudes are present, things are experienced in special ways—we look at them or treat them extraordinarily.

Special attitudes or interests do often seem to characterize people when their attention is directed to certain features of the world rather than others. When my son was a small boy, he and his friends would sometimes look at my art books, and I would hear them giggling. I had a good idea which pictures they were enjoying. But was their enjoyment aesthetic? Attitude theorists would answer no. In his famous book *The Nude*, Kenneth Clark suggests an explanation: The children were treating something nude as something naked. "The nude takes the most sensual and immediately interesting object, the human body, and puts it out of reach of time and desire."[14] The children's attitude was not aesthetic—they had not put the objects beyond time or desire!

We do seem to know at least in a vague, general way what is being asked of us when we are told to consider something aesthetically rather than economically or politically or intellectually, for instance. Considerations of cost or social consequences or truth are temporarily put aside while the appearance or sound is made central. People often report that they go to church for the aesthetic, not for the religious, experience, and we understand them. Most people believe that it is possible to enjoy aesthetically music that was written by a Roman Catholic specifically for an Easter or Christmas mass, even when they do not share the composer's religious beliefs. I have heard people remark that they love to sing hymns even though, as atheists, they would be embarrassed to *speak* those same words, and they explain this by saying that singing is an aesthetic activity, not an intellectual or religious activity, for them. Apparently these people put aside their usual beliefs and attitudes and take an aesthetic point of view. But spelling out in any detail what it means to 'take the aesthetic point of view' is difficult and has generated much debate among aestheticians.

One of the most influential of the aesthetic attitude theorists is Jerome Stolnitz. In a widely discussed article, "The Aesthetic Attitude," he attempts to explain when we have it and what we do, and do not do, when we take such an attitude toward things or events. A variety of attitudes, he claims, determine the way we perceive the world. Since perception is determined by purposes, attention is always selective; we never sense everything that is out there to be sensed. If I need to mop the floor, I look to see if the sponge is worn. I care little about its color. Indeed I'm not even sure, as I sit here in my study, what color my sponge mop is—not just because I use it so rarely, but because I simply haven't been interested in it aesthetically, Stolnitz would say.[15]

Attitudes also guide responses, according to Stolnitz: "[They prepare] us to respond to what we perceive, to act in a way we think will be most effective for achieving our goals."[16] We repress the responses we think will detract or get in the way. Customarily our attitude is "practical" and entails choosing means to particular goals. Because the aesthetic attitude is not goal oriented, it is not customary, according to this theorist.

One of the weaknesses of Stolnitz's view—and with aesthetic experience theories generally—is a failure to give adequate explanation of "practical" attitudes or experiences such as mopping the floor or planning a budget. We must be able to clarify what a practical attitude is if we are to be able to decide whether it is the one people customarily have. More importantly, the practical attitude must be understood fairly well if we are to distinguish it from the aesthetic. Unfortunately, Stolnitz says very little about the practical attitude. When our attitude is practical, he says, we ask about an object, "What can I do with it, and what can it do to me?"[17] This may describe my experience with my mop, but it does not seem to characterize other experiences that I would intuitively identify as "practical"—child rearing or teaching, for example.

More helpful is Stolnitz's contrast of the aesthetic and the practical on the basis of the role of perception. When we respond practically, he says, our goal lies beyond the experience of perceiving the things we're perceiving. Influenced by the view that art is its own justification (the art-for-art's sake view), Stolnitz believes that the aesthetic, unlike the practical, is marked by perceiving for the sake of perceiving. This criterion (perceiving-for-perceiving's-sake) leads to his positive characterization of the aesthetic attitude as "disinterested and sympathetic attention to and contemplation of any object of awareness, for its own sake alone."[18] Here 'disinterested' is the most important term. If we take up an aesthetic attitude toward something, we perceive it in isolation from other things. When we put aside ordinary practical interests, we dwell on the object's "whole nature and character."[19] We are sympathetic and receptive and don't let moral concerns or economic worries, for instance, influence the experience.

The centrality of disinterestedness (not to be confused with *un*interestedness, or lack of interest) has its roots in eighteenth-century aesthetic theories, within both empirical and rationalist philosophic schools. Edmund Burke, discussed earlier in connection with the role of emotion, described experiences of the sublime (experience in which one is awestruck) as "distanced."[20] People put aside ordinary concerns for survival and successful social interaction and enjoy the formal properties—such as color, size, shape, or rhythm—of their surroundings. Normally fire is frightening, but from a safe distance one can enjoy its colors and shape.

In this century the most widely discussed distance theorist has been Edward Bullough. For Bullough, paying attention to formal properties involves distancing ourselves "psychically." We block practical interests or scientific questions that would normally arise. The now-famous example he uses to explain the concept of psychical distance is a performance of *Othello* attended by a jealous husband and a lighting technician. Unable to forget about his own worries, the husband "underdistances" himself—that is, he identifies himself with the title character and hence disregards the properties he would notice if he were having an aesthetic experience—Iago's duplicity, for example. The lighting technician, though attending to what is a legitimate formal property, pays attention to only one feature, with the result that he "overdistances" himself. The mean to be sought is just the right amount of distance—a state in which we "put ourselves out of gear with our practical or actual self," and attend to as many relevant properties as possible.[21]

Undoubtedly Bullough meant his remark about being "out of gear" metaphorically, and it may be unfair to make too much of it. But even as a metaphor for his and similar views, it indicates some serious problems. It makes aesthetic experience seem less psychic and more psychotic.

For Stolnitz and for Bullough, aesthetic experience is marked by contemplation in absence of a goal. The Spanish philosopher José Ortega y Gasset is another supporter of this view.[22] He describes a scene in which a wife, a doctor, a journalist, and a painter are all present at a man's deathbed. Only the painter, who "glances sidewise at the human reality," achieves the aesthetic state. Again the metaphor points to a rather atypical, if not completely abnormal, way of looking at the world, for the painter is the only one who lacks a goal apparently. Stolnitz goes so far as to maintain that art critics do not have aesthetic experiences when they are criticizing art, for they have ulterior motives—writing an article, for instance—while they do what they do. (Might not such an extreme position eliminate Ortega y Gasset's painter and the vast majority of artists who work for a living from the aesthetic group as well?)

If a special form of contemplation is present during aesthetic experiences, people should be able to recognize it when they believe they are having one. Recently I rode the bus from a suburb of Amsterdam into the city's center. As I did so, I paid very close attention to where we were, partly to locate helpful landmarks, partly because the scenery was delightful, partly because I just enjoy following my routes on a map. And I asked myself when, if ever, I was contemplating the scene for itself alone. Distancing, as it is conceived by Burke, Stolnitz, Bullough, and Ortega y Gasset, is a special kind of action; disinterestedness entails an ordinary action done with a special attitude. In either case, the specialness should be recognizable. I thought I was having an aesthetic experience, but definitely did not feel that I was slipping into and out of the aesthetic attitude, or having at one moment an aesthetic experience and then a getting-your-bearings experience.

These theorists might respond that this is just my problem—that I am unable to have aesthetic experiences. But how would they *prove* this? Other writers, J. O. Urmson for instance, have said that when they have what they believe to be genuinely aesthetic experiences they are not aware of anything that might be called the "distancing action" or "the act of assuming the aesthetic attitude."[23] Suppose a newspaper reporter at a deathbed says she is having an aesthetic experience while she takes notes. Are distance theorists justified in saying, "Oh, no, you aren't!"? Suppose some of the people in our movie theater insist that distancing or special attitudes are not part of their aesthetic experience. Do we then have to put them on the non-aesthetic side?

We shall return to problems with aesthetic attitudes in the "Special Focus" section of this chapter. But first we shall look at another special operation explanation of aesthetic experience.

The Role of Thought in Aesthetic Response

Part of the motivation for Sibley's use of taste as a distinctive component of aesthetic response is his belief that this response is a direct, unmediated reaction to something. Thought seems to play little role in such responses. Analyses of aesthetic experience have often stressed feeling and perception, and have played down thought or intellect. As a result, the uniqueness of aesthetic experience has sometimes been accounted for in terms of a suppression or absence of thought.

Suppose you look at a sunset and say, "How vivid those colors are!" Sibley (and Hume and others) claim that making such a judgment is the result of a direct perception—not the result of a thought process. It is like looking at a red apple—we just see that it is red, we do not have to think about it or figure it out. No calculation or deduction is involved.

The same is true of 'vivid' according to this view. You do not have to figure out that the sunset is vivid; you just see that it is. You do not have to say to yourself, "The sun is setting; there's a lot of dust and moisture in the air; therefore the colors I'm looking at must be vivid." Seeing the sunset and seeing that it is vivid happen simultaneously.

In addition to maintaining that noticing aesthetic properties requires the exercise of taste, Sibley also says that aesthetic properties such as intensity or composition are not "condition-governed." People do not reason from a list of non-aesthetic properties—color, size, and location, for example—to a list of aesthetic properties. According to Sibley, "There are no non-aesthetic features which serve in *any* circumstances as logically *sufficient conditions* for applying aesthetic terms. Aesthetic or taste concepts are not in *this* respect condition-governed at all."[24] That is, no matter what non-aesthetic properties I tell you an object possesses (yellow, religious, wavy lines) you will be unable to conclude that there is any aesthetic property that the object has (intense, moving). No condition—such as the color green—governs or determines an aesthetic response. You have to see it for yourself. It is perception, not thought, that results in an aesthetic experience.

Is Sibley correct about this? If so, is this feature unique to aesthetic properties? Does aesthetic experience never depend upon what people *think*?

There are lots of *property terms*—words naming properties—that people use successfully, but for which they cannot state necessary and sufficient conditions. (Try listing them for such common, everyday terms as *chair* or *cup*, for example.) But inability to find even sufficient conditions does, Sibley believes, distinctly mark aesthetic properties. Having dramatically opposed colors does not in every case depend (as it does in Figure 2) on putting paint in two zones, nor does such opposition always result from this kind of arrangement. If we are told that a painting is divided into two zones, we cannot conclude that it has dramatically opposed colors.

Contrast this with a property for which there are sufficient conditions. If a person reads that a car can reach and remain for long periods at a speed of one hundred twenty miles per hour, she knows that it is a fast car. But if she reads that it is blue, shiny, and has a body with curved lines, she cannot conclude that it is beautiful. No matter how many things are added to the list, she has to see it for herself before she knows whether it is beautiful or not.

Even philosophers who do not go along with Sibley's use of taste have been impressed with his claim that aesthetic properties cannot be defined in terms of non-aesthetic properties. Isabel Hungerland, for example, has pointed to what she thinks is a related difference between non-aesthetic and aesthetic properties and hence in people's experiences of them.[25] Consider 'yellow' and 'beautiful'. According to Hungerland, it makes sense to say "The sky *looks* yellow, but it *is not really* yellow." Such constructions ("looks/is not really") work only for non-aesthetic properties, she says. "The sky looks beautiful, but it is not really beautiful" is absurd, she thinks. There is a difference between "is yellow" and "looks yellow" that does not exist for "is beautiful" and "looks beautiful." "Is beautiful" and "looks beautiful" always act like "looks yellow." That is, no claim is made about the actual state of things in either of these phrases.

No description of an object's aesthetic properties commits us to any description of its non-aesthetic properties, according to Hungerland. This is because one's own point of view—one's perceptual standpoint—makes all the difference when an object is described aesthetically. But even if we grant that possession of certain non-aesthetic properties does not guarantee the presence of some aesthetic property (beauty, for instance), other aesthetic properties do seem condition governed. Peter Kivy suggests that having a unified composition is such a property. A person can conclude that a work has this property after hearing a description couched in non-aesthetic terms, without having to see or hear it.[26] This property also passes the "looks/is not really" test: It makes sense to say, "The painting appears to have a unified composition, but it doesn't really." Conditions governing use are not always missing when an aesthetic vocabulary is used. Thus this feature is not a sufficient condition for an aesthetic experience.

There are also many non-aesthetic terms for which it is difficult, if not impossible, to give sufficient conditions. (Consider, for example, *virtuous*, *chair*, or *virus*.) Lack of sufficient conditions does not provide a means of separating the aesthetic. A person's failure to provide sufficient conditions for saying that a movie is "tragic" will not determine where she should sit in our movie theater.

Indeed, many theorists believe that thinking and reasoning are crucial for aesthetic experiences. For example, Nelson Goodman believes that aesthetic experience is one kind of cognitive understanding. (His view that art is a language that must be "read" will be discussed in the next chapter.) Separating emotion and thought—to assume that they are exclusive or incompatible—is a serious mistake, according to Goodman. There is evidence that scientists are emotionally involved with their work and that artists approach their problems intellectually. In aesthetic experience, "The *emotions function cognitively*. The work of art is apprehended through the feelings as well as through the senses."[27]

If this is correct, a movie that is boring will be as likely to shut off aesthetic experience as one that leaves a person emotionally cold. When people are aesthetically involved, they want to study objects more carefully—to think about them, not just perceive qualities or respond emotionally. (Sometimes contemporary art is said to be interesting because it is boring. Carl Andre's work (see Figure 1) has been criticized because it is not boring in interesting ways—that is, it does not refer to its own lack of interest in ways that catch a viewer's attention. Such criticism is quite intellectual!)

Theorists who insist that minds as well as hearts operate in aesthetic experience often stress the point that people seem to *study* aesthetic objects intently. This observation leads to asking whether there is something that is the special object of attention. Could we tell which people are having an aesthetic experience by asking them what they are looking at or listening to—what their special focus is?

SPECIAL FOCUS

The problems encountered in trying to explain aesthetic experience in terms of a special faculty or special operation have led some aestheticians to consider special objects of attention that they believe are typical of it. In "The Myth of the Aesthetic Attitude," George Dickie criticizes special attitude theories.[28] His argument, and the core of the "myth," is essentially this: The concept of an aesthetic attitude depends upon the possibility of distinguishing among various sorts of attending. Dickie insists, however, that there are not various sorts of attending, but only attending or failing to attend. Therefore, the concept of an aesthetic attitude is not viable. The jealous husband and the lighting technician are attending to the play not in ways different from one another or different from someone who is attending aesthetically. Rather, they attend to different things. That is, they do not actually *see* or *look differently* (use their eyes in different ways); they *observe* or *look at different things* (use their eyes normally to look at different things). They are, in fact, not attending to the play at all. The jealous husband thinks mainly about his wife and so sees signs of deception in Desdemona; the technician only watches the lights. 'Distance' does not pick out a special physical or psychological state, according to Dickie. Nor is aesthetic experience even a special kind of experience. That is, it is not to be distinguished from non-aesthetic experience by the nature of the attention involved. Rather, aesthetic experience is special because it involves attending to some things rather than others. It is not *how* we attend, but *what* things we attend to that matters.

But what things are important? Socrates' central question, "What makes things beautiful?", has been modified to "What things must I attend to if I am attending aesthetically?" My definition of 'aesthetic experience' in Chapter 7 will suggest an answer to this question. In his article, Dickie does not give an answer. Others have tried.

Monroe Beardsley has answered that we must attend to the features that we value aesthetically, namely "regional qualities" and "formal unity."[29] Beardsley believes that aesthetic experience is characterized by attention to and pleasure taken in an object's intrinsic qualities and in the way these qualities are related to each other. *Regional qualities* are things such as color, pitch, or rhyme—qualities *in* an object that we perceive as part of the whole that we are experiencing. These qualities are "regional" in the sense that we can actually point to them. That is, they are located in some region of the object—there is a patch of blue in the upper left corner, or a long *a* sound at the end of every other line, or five ascending notes at the beginning of a song. *Formal unity* has to do with the way these qualities are put together—patterns or the organization of parts that an object displays such as repetition or symmetry.

In his review of the movie *High Noon*, for example, Bowsley Crowther described both specific shots and the way they are held together.

> A brilliant assembly of shots . . . holds the tale in taut suspension just before the fatal hour of noon. The issues have been established, the townsfolk have fallen away and the sheriff, alone with his destiny, has sat down at his desk to wait. Over his shoulder Mr. Zimmerman [the director] shows us a white sheet of paper on which is scrawled "last will and testament" by a slowly moving pen. Then he gives us a shot (oft repeated) of the pendulum of the clock.[30]

Regional qualities are features such as over-the-shoulder shots; formal unity includes such things as repeated shots of the clock that give a coherence to the events. If Beardsley is correct, we could ask people in our movie theater what they are looking at. If they say, "Over-the-shoulder shots," we would seat them on the left (aesthetic) side. If they say, "I'm too upset to look at anything," we would send them to the right.

Beardsley's explanation in terms of attention to regional qualities and unity has much in its favor. Certainly there are references to such things in almost all discussions that most people would identify as aesthetic. Here is a musical example:

> The basic sound ideal of the Renaissance was a polyphony of independent voices; the sound ideal of the Baroque was a firm bass and a florid treble, held together by unobtrusive harmony. The idea of a musical texture consisting of a single melody supported by accompanying harmonies was not in itself new.[31]

And in the following passage, lack of reference to either regional qualities or the way they are organized does belie a non-aesthetic intent:

> The name of one man is indissolubly linked with the Zuder Zee project, that of Cornelius Lely, who devoted a large part of his life to it. As early as 1891, Lely, who was then still an engineer with the Zuder Zee Association, established by private initiative in 1886, was busy surveying the possibilities.[32]

Beardsley's view is also reinforced in the history of Western aesthetics. What Beardsley calls "regional qualities" are essentially the same things that others have referred to as "formal qualities" or "intrinsic qualities valued for themselves alone" and similar language. The term 'regional qualities' is broad, and we need to specify which are most aesthetically relevant—something I hope to do when I present my own theory of the aesthetic in Chapter 7. In the eighteenth century, the philosopher Edmund Burke gave light, vastness, infinity, difficulty, smoothness, delicacy, color, size, and grandeur as examples of qualities that promote aesthetic experience. Ortega y Gasset suggested lights, shadows, and chromatic values. Stolnitz generalizes by referring to perceptual qualities valued for their own sakes. We find scores of similar lists or generalizations in aesthetic theories.

The second feature named by Beardsley, "formal unity," has an even longer history. It appears in the *Poetics* of Aristotle, where he argues that the plot of a good tragedy must have as its subject an action that is clearly developed and ties together the beginning, middle, and end. Everything in the play that is needed is there, and, even more crucial for unity, everything that is there is needed. There are no loose ends to distract from the central theme. Lengthy discussions of the "three unities" of drama—place, time, and action—throughout the Middle Ages and Renaissance show how seriously this concept was taken then. In the eighteenth century it was still central to many aesthetic systems. Frances Hutcheson, for example, insisted that the foundation of aesthetic value lies in what he called "uniformity in variety."[33]

Others have used the term 'organic unity'. Aristotle said that like a plant, a work of art is an intricate arrangement of parts, all of which contribute to the whole. The roots, stem, leaves, and blossom are all necessary. So a work of art—a play, for instance—is made up of parts, all of which ideally contribute to the whole. Later writers (Coleridge, for example) emphasized that in an organism, the interconnection and interarrangement of parts comes from within the organism; it is not imposed from the outside. Thus successful works of art can be said to have an organic unity—that is, the arrangement of parts seems to have come from the work itself, not to have been superimposed by a creator or viewer.

As with most terms with a long history, 'unity' is often ambiguous, and thus it is not always clear what we are being told or what is being pointed to when the term is used to describe something. "It's good because it's unified," would probably not have satisfied Socrates' antagonists any more than it would ours. Theorists who rely on this notion have the task of explaining what it means.

SUMMARY

Aesthetic issues concerning viewers have been the topics of several contemporary philosophical debates. Sometimes the viewer's experience is explained in terms of a special faculty such as taste, and the aesthetic is characterized as a special sensitivity or perceptiveness. Aesthetic experience has also been explained by the presence of special attitudes that people assume in which everyday, practical concerns are put aside or in which thought gives way to emotion. Other theorists prefer explanations in which a viewer's focus is directed to special features such as formal qualities or unity.

Some of these theories have suggested ways in which one might accomplish the task set at the beginning of this chapter (determining if someone is having an aesthetic experience). However, readers may not yet be completely satisfied. After discussion of some other aesthetic issues, I will propose a solution in Chapter 7.

| NOTES

1. Siegfried Kracauer, *Theory of Film* (Oxford: Oxford University Press, 1960), p. 159.

2. David Hume, *Of the Standard of Taste, and Other Essays* (Indianapolis: Bobbs-Merrill, 1965).

3. Frank Sibley, "Aesthetic Concepts," *Philosophical Review* 68 (1959): 421–50; and "Aesthetic and Nonaesthetic," *Philosophical Review* 74 (1965): 135–59.

4. Meyer Schapiro, *Vincent Van Gogh* (New York: Harry N. Abrams, 1950), p. 104. Reprinted by permission of the publisher. All rights reserved.

5. Sibley uses and confuses 'term', 'property', and 'concept'. I shall restrict my discussion to 'property'.

6. For a good discussion of this point, see Mary Mothersill, *Beauty Restored* (Oxford: Clarendon Press, 1984), pp. 100–177.

7. Elizabeth Belfiore has argued that *catharsis* has been overemphasized in discussions of Aristotle's theory of tragedy. See "Pleasure, Tragedy, and Aristotelian Psychology," *Classical Quarterly* 35 (1985): 349–61.

8. Edmund Burke, *A Philosophical Inquiry into the Ideas of the Sublime and the Beautiful*, ed. J. T. Boulton (London: Routledge and Kegan Paul, 1958). (Originally published 1757.)

9. Colin Radford, "How Can We Be Moved by the Fate of Anna Karenina?", *Proceedings of the Aristotelian Society* suppl. vol. 49 (1975): 67–93.

10. Michael Westen agrees with me. See his response to the Radford article in *Proceedings of the Aristotelian Society* 49 (1975).

11. Susan Feagin, "The Pleasures of Tragedy," *American Philosophical Quarterly* 20 (1983): 95-104.

12. Gary Iseminger, "How Strange a Sadness," *Journal of Aesthetics and Art Criticism* no. 1 (1983): 81-82.

13. For a further discussion, see Marcia M. Eaton, "Strange Kind of Sadness," *Journal of Aesthetics and Art Criticism* 39, no. 1 (Fall 1980): 51-63.

14. Kenneth Clark, *The Nude; A Study of Ideal Art* (London: John Murray, 1956), p. 22.

15. Stolnitz emphasizes the extent to which the passive, "blank tablet" model of the human mind is inadequate, and he is right to do so. However, I think he goes too far in the other direction. We do not simply decide to pay attention to this, but not to that. Some things about our environments call attention to themselves in spite of the particular purpose we have at a given moment. If fire breaks out in my kitchen, I notice it even though the goal of the moment is mopping that floor. Thus I shall discuss Stolnitz in terms of attitudes *affecting* rather than *determining* our perception.

16. Jerome Stolnitz, *Aesthetics and the Philosophy of Art* (Boston: Houghton Mifflin, 1960), p. 33.

17. Ibid., p. 33.

18. Ibid., p. 35.

19. Ibid., p. 35.

20. Edmund Burke, *A Philosophical Inquiry.*

21. Edward Bullough, " 'Psychical Distance' as a Factor in Art and an Aesthetic Principle," *British Journal of Psychology* 5 (1912): 80.

22. José Ortega y Gasset, "The Dehumanization of Art," reprinted in *A Modern Book of Esthetics*, ed. Melvin Rader (New York: Holt, Rinehart and Winston, 1960), pp. 411-19.

23. For further discussion of this point, see J. O. Urmson, "What Makes a Situation Aesthetic?", *Proceedings of the Aristotelian Society* suppl. vol. 31 (1957): 75-92.

24. Sibley, "Aesthetic Concepts," p. 423.

25. Isabel Hungerland, "Once Again, Aesthetic and Non-Aesthetic," *Journal of Aesthetics and Art Criticism* vol. 27 (1968): 285-95.

26. Peter Kivy, "Aesthetic Aspects and Aesthetic Qualities," *Journal of Philosophy* 65, no. 4 (1968): 85-93.

27. Nelson Goodman, *Languages of Art* (Indianapolis, Ind.: Bobbs-Merrill, 1960), p. 248.

28. George Dickie, "The Myth of the Aesthetic Attitude," *American Philosophical Quarterly* 1, no. 1 (1964): 56–65.

29. Monroe Beardsley, "The Aesthetic Point of View," in *Perspectives in Education*, ed. Howard E. Kiefer and Milton K. Munitz (Albany, N.Y.: 1970), p. 10.

30. Bowsley Crowther, review of *High Noon*, in *New York Times Film Reviews*, ed. George Amberg (New York: Quadrangle Books, 1971), p. 271.

31. Donald Jay Gould, *A History of Western Music* (New York: Norton, 1980), p. 300.

32. *Room at Last*! (The Hague: Ministry of Transport and Public Works, 1980), p. 9.

33. Frances Hutcheson, *An Inquiry Concerning Beauty, Order, Harmony, Design*, ed. Peter Kivy (The Hague: Martinus Nijhoff, 1973).

CHAPTER 4

Art and Language

> *"You know, uncle, I never see the beauty of those pictures which you say are so much praised. They are a language I do not understand. I suppose there is some relation between pictures and nature which I am too ignorant to feel—just as you see what a Greek sentence stands for which means nothing to me."*
>
> Dorothea, *Middlemarch*, by George Eliot

For centuries, thinkers have been interested in the symbolic character of the objects of artistic and aesthetic experience. Sometimes discussions of "art as symbol" have concentrated on the revelation of mythic or unconscious human experience. More recently in philosophical aesthetics, discussions have concentrated on problems suggested by the remark that Dorothea makes to her uncle in the quotation from *Middlemarch*. She thinks that she fails to understand some pictures that she looks at (and thus fails to have an aesthetic experience) because she does not understand their "language." She feels the way she does when someone speaks to her in a language that she does not speak; she simply doesn't "get" what is going on. Others say the same sort of thing about other art forms—about music or dance or films, for instance. Some people say that classical music is "Greek" to them; others feel that the movements in a dance or a sequence of frames in a movie must be related to something, but fail to get the connection.

Within contemporary analytic circles, philosophers are interested in how aesthetic symbol systems can be compared and contrasted with other kinds of linguistic systems. Particular attention is paid to whether or how works of art stand for things in the world, as words do, and to whether and how works of art say things about the world, as sentences do. In this chapter we shall examine the extent to which having an aesthetic experience depends upon something like knowing the language in which objects are "written."

Clearly language is central to literary art forms. The medium of literature is words that already exist within a natural language. Literature has special linguistic problems, primarily those of meaning and truth. Some of these problems also arise with respect to non-literary arts. The question of truth will be discussed later in this chapter; meaning is a topic of Chapter 6. We shall begin by seeing whether visual and musical arts function as languages. Do we "read" them? Must we know the language in which they are "written" in order to understand them? Is art really a universal language? Or, as for Dorothea, are some works of art "Greek" to us?

Both sights and sounds can be used to form symbol systems that function as mini-languages. The visual language of often illiterate hoboes provides a fascinating example of modern ideograms.

Hit the road quick!

Good place to catch a train

Good place for handout

Church bells can be used to relay important messages to distant farmsteads; sirens can warn us to get out of the way.

The *Iconologica* of Cesare Ripe, a famous reference work, contains hundreds of examples of visual symbols used by medieval painters. It is, without stretching the comparison too much, very like a dictionary.[1] Dogs, he points out, stand for loyalty; a man with arrows stuck in him is St. Sebastian. Ripe's reference work shows that medieval painters consciously used configurations within their works to convey definite meanings to their usually illiterate viewers. Just as we cannot comprehend an ode written in a foreign language unless we understand the words, we cannot interpret the significance of the presence of certain shapes unless we know what they stand for. Unlike medieval audiences who "knew the language," we will not know that the man with the arrows stuck in him is St. Sebastian (know what that configuration represents) without being told.

We find similar, though fewer, examples of this need to decipher codes in music. Certain groups of notes may, as they do in Prokofiev's *Peter and the Wolf*, refer to the wolf or Peter or the cat. In some Eastern music, the note groupings are often as fixed as the dog-shape has been in Western painting; for example, some musical phrases almost always stand for a tree or a pond. Western composers also use music to represent properties of the things referred to. For example, Handel makes crooked places straight:

the crook-ed straight,

The music theorist Deryck Cooke argues that music in general works like a language. He believes, for example, that in Western music major keys are used to signify happiness, minor keys sorrow.[2]

Recently philosophers of art have become more and more interested in a set of problems that a facile look at a painting may conceal. We seem to have no trouble saying what many paintings represent. In the picture *The Way You Hear It Is the Way You Sing It*, we see a woman looking at a piece of paper, presumably singing the song that appears on it (see Figure 3). The words at the top of the page the old woman holds appear to be the ones that are to be sung to the tune written at the bottom of it. The words and notes are a bit blurred, but they can be made out, and art historians have identified the song. (More will be said about the painting later.) In any case, we can easily recognize the page as a song, just as we recognize the people, furniture, bagpipes, dog, and walls depicted in the painting. But problems arise when we try to define 'representation'. What does it mean to say that this painting represents a woman or a dog or bagpipes? Does the page the woman is holding represent a song? What, if anything, does the verse represent?

For a long time Western philosophers and art theorists believed that visual representation was a kind of imitation. According to this view, the white area in the middle of the painting is said to represent a sheet of music because it looks like one. The shape next to it represents a woman because it resembles a woman. Friends of Jan Steen, the artist, could probably have said exactly which woman it looked like.

But closer analysis exposes problems with explaining representation in terms of resemblance. That is, it is not enough to say that a picture represents something because it resembles that thing. Two thinkers, the art historian and theorist E. H. Gombrich and the philosopher Nelson Goodman have pointed out weaknesses in resemblance theories of representation. Both prefer theories of representation that involve treating art as a kind of language.

Goodman has shown that there are important logical differences between representation and resemblance.[3] Two dining room chairs resemble, but do not represent, one another. If a painting resembles a horse, then the horse must also resemble the painting, but a painting may represent a horse without the horse in turn representing the painting of it. If two things resemble a third thing, then they must resemble one another; not so for representation. Two paintings may

Figure 3 Jan Steen (1626–1679), *The Way You Hear It Is the Way You Sing It*, Foundation Johan Maurits van Nassau/Mauritshuis Museum, the Hague. Used by permission.

represent George Washington but not represent one another. Thus Goodman believes that the representing relation must be explained in terms of something other than resemblance.

Gombrich has dismissed a resemblance, or imitation, theory of representation on psychological grounds.[4] He believes that when an artist undertakes to represent something, it is not a matter of putting something on paper that matches or copies what is seen. Instead, Gombrich thinks visual representation involves manipulating signs—"schemas," he calls them—that will be recognized as standing for particular things. A stick drawing of a woman does not resemble a woman. It can be used to represent a woman, nonetheless, because it works as a sign for one.

Both writers urge us, to use words of Gombrich, to treat the phrase 'the language of art' as "more than a loose metaphor."[5] Following their lead, contemporary aestheticians have increasingly studied the extent to which artistic and aesthetic symbol systems are essentially linguistic in nature. Visual and musical art certainly *can* transmit messages. But do they *always* do this? Is it correct to say that all art, not just literature, is essentially linguistic in nature?

LANGUAGE IN NON-LITERARY ARTS

Linguistic Features of Art

One way to see how strong a connection exists between art and language is to consider those features that any system must possess if it is correctly to be called a language. If visual and musical art forms have those features, then, and only then, will it be correct to say that they are, or at least sometimes function as, languages. Only then will we see if the phrase "the language of art" is more than a loose metaphor.

Every language, whether a natural language like English, or a formal language like algebra, has a vocabulary—a set of signs that can stand for something. The language must also have a syntax—rules for putting the vocabulary items together. Finally there must be a semantics, which provides a method for saying what the items thus joined mean.

Much of the attention that has been given to construing art as language has concentrated on what might constitute its vocabulary. Philosophers of language, such as H. P. Grice, often distinguish between natural and non-natural signs.[6] *Natural signs* are associated with what they signify; smoke is a natural sign of fire. Non-natural signs have a conventional association; the word *dog* is a non-natural sign for four-legged animals of a certain genus and species.

Philosophers of art have debated over whether art has a natural or non-natural vocabulary. Does the shape that represents a dog in Steen's painting bear a natural relation to dogs? Or must we learn via conventions that shapes of that sort stand for dogs—much in the way that we learn that the shape 'dog' stands for a certain kind of animal? As we shall see later in this chapter, Gombrich and Goodman favor the non-natural, or conventional, view.

The American philosopher C. S. Peirce was one of the first to try to make another kind of distinction among different sorts of signs, and some art theorists have used his classification. He identified three kinds:

Icon: "a sign which refers to the object that it denotes merely by virtue of characters of its own"

Index: "a sign which refers to the object that it denotes by virtue of being affected by that object"

Symbol: "a sign which is constituted a sign merely or mainly by the fact that it is used and understood as such"[7]

An architect's model of a building is an *icon*: it represents the building by sharing essential properties with it. Spots are an *index* of measles because they appear as an effect of that disease. The word *dog* is a *symbol*, in Peirce's view, because only people who already understand its use will know what it signifies. Obviously the divisions are not clean. Onomatopoetic words—words whose sound suggests their sense, such as *hiss*—have both natural (or iconic) and non-natural (or symbolic) features. (Dogs do not say "bow-wow" in French, for example.) The hobo sign for "good place to catch a train" shares some visual characteristics with what it signifies, but it also succeeds because it is used conventionally to refer to a place.

Clearly in Peirce's classification, the first kind of a sign, an icon, would be the sort emphasized in a resemblance theory of representation. According to this theory, the woman-shape in Figure 3 is an icon, for it bears a natural resemblance to what it signifies. So it is not surprising that icons have received a great deal of attention in art history and theory.[8]

The art historian Erwin Panofsky suggested that art icons can be studied on three levels.[9] On the *iconic* level, a picture stands for something because it resembles that thing. On the *iconographic* level, a picture stands for something via recognized practices, for example, a dog stands for loyalty. On the *iconological* level, a picture stands for an idea, expressing the relation between truth and beauty, for example, or makes metaphysical claims about the reality of the physical world.

Panofsky and other art historians have primarily been interested in artistic meaning at the iconological and iconographical levels. They point out, for example, that the presence of a dog in a painting signals that the scene presented is one in which the activity is virtuous. One of the great contributions of E. H. Gombrich is that he has shown how complex art is at the most basic level. He has opened up serious philosophical questions about the iconic (resembling) nature of signs in the visual arts. He asks not how a shape can stand for virtue but, more fundamentally, how a shape can stand for a *dog*.

Before we look at Gombrich's view, however, let's think more about why the drive to liken art to language is so strong. Partly it is because of the widespread use of expressions such as "language of art," "read the notes," "understand the message of the painting," and "meaning." But the comparison of art to language also stems from the feeling that, as with literature, visual art and music *signify* something—for example, feelings, as we discussed in Chapter 2—and this leads naturally to the belief that an artwork must be or contain *signs* of something. The use of a complex notation in music, which must be learned much as we learn to read words, supports the belief that music communicates via a language.

Another reason that art lends itself to explanation in linguistic terms is that both the visual and performing arts are so often discussed not just in terms of vocabulary but also in terms of syntax and semantics—features that a language must have.

Look again at our painting in Figure 3. In it we find a variety of marks—

words, musical notes, and visual shapes. Our ability to intepret the painting depends upon our ability to recognize the marks for what they are and to relate them properly to one another. Suppose that we could read the song the woman is singing; it is an old Dutch nursery rhyme. We could then say that we recognize, or interpret, three kinds of marks or signs.

VOCABULARY

words	notes	shapes
you	C	woman-shape
hear	G	page-shape
sing	F#	dog-shape

For each kind of language, there is a syntáx. The words are put together in a certain order, as are the musical notes and the visual shapes. In each case, the order or snytax could be changed. For example, the verse could read, "Sing you it the way you hear it?" The notes could be written backwards. The dog might be on the chair holding the paper and the woman sitting on the floor. Or without the order being changed, syntactic alterations could be made by changing individual vocabulary items. "Hear" and "sing" could be changed to "pour" and "drink." The final note could be raised an octave. The curious dog could be changed to a yapping, distressed dog.

Such changes would make a difference in our interpretation in each category (natural language, music, painting) because a semantics exists for each. The words have an assigned meaning. Major keys are appropriate to praise, and dogs signal loyalty or virtue in general. In this painting all symbol systems unite to present us with the same message: Here's a middle-class home in which robust but decent activity is the rule. (This is not, of course, the only message.)

We must, however, not be too hasty in accepting the claim that musical and visual arts have the requisite vocabulary, syntax, and semantics. If music has them, it has them only so far as the making of particular sounds is concerned. There is more to music, most people believe, than just playing the right notes.[10] Furthermore, Cooke's claim that there is a language of music—with major keys signifying joy and minor keys sorrow, for instance—applies only to a subset of musical experiences. It does seem true of Baroque music but less so of contemporary compositions.

Painting, too, only occasionally exhibits vocabulary, syntax, or semantics in any clear-cut way. I have spoken loosely about the woman-shape in our painting. But is this shape like a letter, a word, or a sentence? Should we instead look for our vocabulary in brush strokes? Do Steen and his Dutch contemporary Vermeer speak the same or different visual languages? Presumably criteria of the same and different languages will be connected with vocabulary and ways of putting items from it together. If the languages of Steen and Vermeer are the same, then there should be some way of discovering what in Vermeer stands for a woman and of saying whether it is the same or a variation in Steen's paintings.

Both painting and music, even if we see in them some similarities to what might be called a vocabulary (dog = loyalty; minor key = sorrow), lack any semblance of connecting words that establish logical relations. These connecting words—such as *and*, *if/then*, and *either/or*—are used to establish relationships between sentences: "If a dog barks, then trouble is brewing."

And music and painting lack the even more rudimentary linguistic feature of negation. No painting by itself, without a lot of accompanying words, can say, "This is not how Toledo looked"; nor can a piece of music tell us, "This is not how I felt when my daughter died." In language, two predicates, *red* and *big*, for instance, can be attributed to the same thing. But suppose we have two different views of Salisbury Cathedral or two songs about the Danube. If we treat them as different predicates and put them together, we usually only get something incoherent.

We do not want to stretch the metaphor "the language of art" too far. With such problems as lack of clearly identifiable vocabulary, syntax, semantics, or logical words in mind, we will now look more closely at the theories of Gombrich and Goodman to see how and why they interpret the metaphor the way they do.

Gombrich's Theory of Representation

Gombrich's reasons for taking the metaphor "the language of art" seriously, for thinking, as I have put it, that the necessary features for being a language are present in art, rest on his recognition that objects in art can be used to refer to things beyond themselves. This view is by no means radical or novel. What makes Gombrich's contribution to art history and philosophy so important is his demonstration that this reference does not depend upon resemblance. Indeed *languages* seem to arise precisely when we get beyond the level of association based on resemblance or natural cause (icons and indexes, for Peirce) and arrive at the level of what Peirce calls *symbols*—conventional signs.

The naive view of representation that Gombrich wants to dispel is that visual artists look at things and then try to reproduce them on paper or in stone. As he puts it, it is a mistake to think that artists try to match what they see by making the proper sort of mark. Rather, "making comes before matching." Artists do not come to their work with an "innocent eye," but use schemata or vocabularies that have developed across the years. Herein lies his reason for viewing art as linguistic in nature.

Consider the drawing of a face. Why do most of us begin with a circle? It cannot be because we have seen circular, or even spherical, heads. We draw a circle because this is the schema, or word, we have learned for visually depicting faces. Of course, skilled artists do not stop with a circle; they modify it until it represents George instead of Martha Washington. But the refinements come about through a manipulation of what has been *made* (the circle), not by first attempting to match what is seen. The existence of "How to Draw" books indicates that becoming an artist, like becoming a musician or a poet, requires learning a language.

In *The Sense of Order*, Gombrich provides his own summary for his famous book *Art and Illusion:*

> In *Art and Illusion* I have tried to show "why art has a history." I gave psychological reasons for the fact that the rendering of nature cannot be achieved by an untutored individual, however gifted, without the support of a tradition. I found the reasons in the psychology of perception, which explains why we cannot simply "transcribe" what we see and have to resort to methods of trial and error in the slow process of "making and matching," and "schema and correction." Given the aim of creating a convincing picture of reality, this is the way the arts will "evolve"; the aim in its turn must depend on the function assigned to the visual arts in a particular culture such as that of ancient Greece.[11]

By the "process of 'making and matching,' and 'schema and correction'," Gombrich is referring to the sort of activity described above—turning circles into pictures of people. Gombrich rejects a resemblance theory of representation in favor of a substitution theory, where items substitute for or stand for things depending on our needs and purposes. Circles are our substitute for heads when we draw people, just as a stick can substitute for a spoon when children play house. The circle and the stick serve their purpose not so much because they are good *resemblances*, but because they are good *substitutes*.[12]

Gombrich retains an element of what I referred to earlier as 'natural' or 'non-conventional meaning', for he argues that human psychology plays an important role in the symbols that are used. Our tendency to see human faces in everything from clouds to automobile fronts, for example, indicates a non-arbitrary aspect of representation that he probably would not believe is present in musical scores and written texts. Pictures are "stand-ins" that *stand for* things. Nonetheless, representational pictures are more like symbols than they are like icons or indexes, Gombrich thinks, and thus he believes that art is a language.

Goodman's View of Representation

The other important writer who takes "the language of art" metaphor seriously is Nelson Goodman. Like Gombrich, he rejects the resemblance theory of representation, but he favors denotation over substitution. The word *dog* denotes dogs; it refers or points to a particular kind of animal. Goodman believes that pictures, like words, stand for things not because they are used in place of those things, but simply because we learn what they point to. There is nothing natural or non-conventional about the way pictures denote things. Like words and notes, the woman-shape in Steen's painting stands for a woman because it is an element in a symbol system we have learned to read, and in that system that particular shape stands for a woman.

Goodman believes that a visual symbol system such as Steen used in his painting is every bit as arbitrary or conventional as a musical score or written text. We *feel* that the woman-shape is somehow less arbitrary, more dependent on a natural relationship between the shape and the woman than notes or words are to what they stand for. But this feeling is due, he argues, to habituation. To use a term from his work in the philosophy of science, such shapes are so firmly "entrenched" in our culture that they have taken on the illusion of realism—the illusion of illusion, if you will. To an observer outside of our culture, the shapes we use will no more look like what they stand for than theirs do to us. Goodman even claims that the "laws" of perspective are not visual laws at all, but conventional practices.[13]

Goodman's views on the conventionality of representation are hotly debated.[14] Some people have mustered anthropological evidence for the recognized superiority of Western perspectival methods. They maintain that once people have been exposed to them, they invariably prefer the Western laws of perspective to obtain realistic rendering of nature. Others insist that, at the very least, visual relationships between parts—eyes above nose above mouth, for example—must be matched if a painting is to be realistic. The philosopher Patrick Maynard, for instance, believes that paintings can only be realistic if they capture "sensorily vivid representations of a particular sort of characteristic," such as a long nose or a moving train.[15] Richard Wollheim, though agreeing that the resemblance theory of representation is wrong, believes nonetheless that looking at pictures is not like unraveling codes. We seem to see pictures simultaneously as configurations and non-conventional depictions, he says.[16]

Another way of contesting Goodman's theory is by insisting that in painting, unlike literature, *seeing* plays a central role and that this accounts for the significant difference between the two. Roger Scruton claims, "If a picture of a man is to be properly appreciated it must at least be possible to see the picture as a man (to see a man in the picture)."[17] This simply is not the case with reading or deciphering codes. A poem may vividly depict an old woman; it may even produce a vivid image of an old woman in my imagination. However, we would not say that the words on the page resemble an old woman. We do want to say that in Steen's painting there is something that looks like an old woman, Scruton would insist.

One can disagree with the conventional aspect of Goodman's theory and still retain the denotational aspect. That is, one can insist that not just any sign can be used to stand for something—that the way the signs look makes a difference. (Circles may do a better job than figure-eights for faces, for instance.) Still one can agree with Goodman that more than the look matters; we must learn what a sign denotes, or stands for, just as we must learn what a word denotes, or stands for. Successful representation is denotative or referential in painting just as it is in music and language. Shapes like words or notes stand for something beyond themselves, and we must know the system before we can get from the sign to what it signifies.

Nonetheless, painting consists of a special kind of denotation, and herein lies a crucial difference between it and the other arts. This difference is indicated by a distinction that exists between what Goodman calls "allographic" and "autographic" art forms.[18] *Allographic art*, including, for example, poems and symphonies, is work of which there is or can be more than one copy. Both you and I can possess *Paradise Lost* and the newly discovered organ works of Bach. *Autographic art* is art for which only one embodiment exists. Only the Rijksmuseum in Amsterdam has Rembrandt's *Nightwatch*. Copies or reproductions of it certainly do exist—but they are not the real thing. For economic, historic, or sentimental reasons we may care if we possess *The Waste Land* written in T. S. Eliot's own hand or Mahler's Second Symphony with conductor Bernhard Haitinck's marginal comments. But as long as all the words and notes are in the right places, we indisputably have the real thing no matter who wrote it out. (More will be said about the ontological status of art—what constitutes a *real* work of art—in Chapter 5.) Only the object produced by Rembrandt is the actual *Nightwatch*.

This distinction grows out of an essential difference between the kinds of symbol systems involved in visual art, on the one hand, and music and literature, on the other hand, according to Goodman. He believes that some symbol systems—musical scores and literary texts, for instance—capture the identifying features of works. That is, the things that make something a performance of Mahler's Second Symphony and not of Beethoven's Ninth are present in the score. Of course, individual performances of Mahler's Second will differ. But the features that can differ and still give us a performance of the same symphony are not in the score. All the necessary features—everything that must be there if we are to identify the performances as performances of the same thing—are present and denoted by the score. With literary and musical works we can go from score to performance and back to the score. As a friend reads a poem from her text, I can write out a new text that allows another friend to repeat exactly the same poem. Most of us cannot do that with a piece of music, but musicians are trained to do it; even for long, complicated works like Mahler's Second Symphony, it is theoretically possible to do so, especially with the aid of recording equipment.

We cannot reproduce paintings via a text or score, argues Goodman. *No* changes are allowable in the *Nightwatch* without its becoming a different work of art. The identifying features here simply cannot be captured in a score or text, and this makes pictorial symbol systems special. Unlike those for music and literature, pictorial symbol systems are not what Goodman calls 'notational'.

As I suggested earlier, one approach to the question of whether "the language of art" is more than a loose metaphor is to see if art possesses those features considered necessary and sufficient for language. Goodman believes that a necessary feature of language is *repeatability*. We must be able to go from one utterance (or performance) to text (or score) and back again. Thus he concludes that representational painting is not a language. It lacks the notational features of languages that make repetition possible.

A genuine notational system has both syntactical and semantical requirements. Syntactical requirements demand that each mark must be unique and distinguishable from all others and must stand for only one thing.[19] In written English, one must be able to recognize the letters *d*, *o*, and *g* and distinguish them from *c*, *a*, and *t*. Semantical requirements ensure that *dog* must stand for only one kind of animal. If I write *dog*, you must be able to pick out one sort of animal and show it to a third person who can then again write *dog*. We must be able to go unambiguously from utterance (or performance) to text (or score) and back again ad infinitum.

The controversy generated by Goodman's work here primarily concerns whether he is correct that all the important necessary or identifying characteristics of a musical work are captured by or in a score. Tempo, for example, does not meet his notational requirements. If I write *allegro* and you play a piece rather quickly, another transcriber may identify it as *allegretto*. Thus tempo becomes a non-essential feature of music for Goodman. Many people believe that this is sheer nonsense; a performance of Chopin's *Minute* Waltz that took three days, even if all the notes were played correctly, would not be a performance of it at all. Nor does the existing notation for playing triplets against eighth notes capture what actually goes on in several measures in, for example, Beethoven's Piano Sonata in G Minor.

Other people believe that Goodman simply does not understand what music is. That is, they feel that music is not captured in a score; it is what we hear and experience and that is not the same as marks on a page. (I shall say more about *where* music is in Chapter 5.) In Chapter 2 we saw that Suzanne Langer believes that music symbolizes human experience, but she did not have in mind the relationship between a score and the notes played in compliance with it. She believes that music lacks dictionary-type references. "We are always free to fill its subtle articulate forms with any meaning that fits them; that is, it may convey an idea of anything conceivable in its logical image," she writes.[20] If what is important about music cannot be captured in notation, then the distinction between autographic and allographic art does not point to a significant difference between music and visual art as Goodman thinks it does.

From the opposite direction, some people have claimed that some representations do seem fully notatable. I have made several cross-stitch calendars and pillowcases that represent flowers, snowmen, or young girls, and I do them by following a pattern that meets all of the requirements for a notational system. Different kinds of marks on a pattern tell me where to make yellow Xs and where to make green Xs so that representations of daisies appear on the pillowcase. I can then give the pillowcase to my mother, and she can reproduce the pattern. This seems to be as repeatable as a poem or sonata. Thus notatability is not always a feature of music or never a feature of visual representation. It does not separate visual from non-visual art.

Before we turn to art and truth, let's summarize what we've said about artistic symbol systems. Philosophers who have regarded art as a kind of language think that artworks refer to something beyond themselves and seem to do this by way of vocabulary, syntax, and semantics. E. H. Gombrich and Nelson Goodman have pointed to important characteristics that the non-literary arts share with linguistic symbol systems.

Others think that although the phrase "the language of art" may be more than a loose metaphor, it is still a metaphor. It is not clear exactly what counts as vocabulary in some paintings, for example. Furthermore, there are important differences between seeing a printed page and reading it. Even Gombrich has written, "We are aware, in the Alhambra, of the delights that await us wherever our eye may wish to settle, but we do not start pursuing or unraveling every scroll."[21] Like Richard Wollheim, he is aware of a difference between reading the words, "The way you hear it is the way you sing it," hearing the notes, and recognizing a picture of a woman about to sing a song.

ART AND TRUTH

In the discussion of the visual arts, the main problems concern the presence or absence of a language. In the literary arts, we assume that a language is present, and thus philosophers concentrate on the concepts of *meaning* and *truth*. Questions of whether works of art have a meaning that can be discovered and agreed upon or whether truth contributes to the value of a literary work will be discussed in later chapters. Here we are interested in whether artworks can be said to be true or false. We shall first look at truth in one literary form, fiction, and then return to the non-literary arts to see how truth is involved there.

Truth and Fiction

The phrase "fictional truth" is apparently contradictory. Since works of fiction announce themselves as not true, as dealing with people who never existed or things that never happened—"any similarity to actual persons living or dead is purely coincidental"—how can any sentences in them be treated as anything but false?

Fictional sentences have been treated in a variety of ways. Many philosophers have taken sentences from works of fiction as clear cases of a sort of sentence that they find very puzzling: sentences containing non-referring names or terms. Consider this sentence, taken from Dickens's *A Christmas Carol*: "Scrooge followed to the window, desperate in his curiosity." Since there never was a

Scrooge, the name is non-referential—there is no one, and has never been anyone, to whom that name (or any description of him in *A Christmas Carol*) refers.

One group of philosophers believes that such sentences are simply false.[22] "Scrooge followed to the window," is an abbreviation, they say, for the longer sentence, "There was a person named 'Scrooge' and he followed to the window." Any sentence about Scrooge implicitly states that he exists; he does not; therefore, the sentence is false.

Another group argues that such sentences simply lack truth-value; that is, they are neither true *nor* false.[23] These people believe that groups of words that include non-referring names or descriptions are not full-fledged or well-formed declarative sentences. Thus they think that attribution of either truth or falsity to them is impossible. It would be like trying to attribute truth or falsity to a question or a command or to a non-sentence—a group of words without a subject or predicate, for example.

A third group tries to bring the complicated machinery of possible-world theory to the rescue.[24] Fictional works create possible worlds in which readers can distinguish what is true from what is false. In *A Christmas Carol*, for example, Dickens presents a possible world in which Scrooge is a miser who becomes a philanthropist, not a philanthropist who becomes a miser.

Yet another solution has been suggested by philosophers who think that in discussions of fiction, truth or falsity is simply irrelevant.[25] In literature, they claim, language is not used as it is standardly used in everyday communication. Hence these people think that it is a mistake to make standard assessments of them. We really don't care whether the sentence "Scrooge followed to the window, desperate in his curiosity" is actually true or false. When we read *A Christmas Carol* and other works of fiction, we put aside our normal concerns about truth, they claim.

In addition to containing sentences with non-referring names, fiction also has perfectly ordinary sentences that do refer to things we know exist or existed. For example, in *The Day of the Scorpion*, Paul Scott writes, "There are still Muslims in Ranpur but the days are gone when the great festivals of the Id al-fitr and the I al-Adzha could fill the mosques with thousands of the faithful from the city and the surrounding villages of the plain."[26] Fictional works also contain what we call abstractions or generalizations. For example, the opening sentence of Tolstoy's *Anna Karenina* claims, "Happy families are all alike; every unhappy family is unhappy in its own way." What are we to do with sentences like these?

Philosophers interested primarily in the logic of non-referring names (the first two groups mentioned earlier) have nothing to say about "ordinary" or abstract sentences that appear in fiction. Members of the third and fourth groups would handle such sentences in the same way as non-referential sentences. If Scott and Tolstoy have created possible worlds for us, then we, as readers, assume that in these worlds there are not many Muslims in Ranpur, or that happy and unhappy families are as Tolstoy says they are. If we dismiss the question of truth or falsity, then the issue of the truth of the sentences about Ranpur or marriage does not arise. We do not rush to get a book on the religious demography of India as we read *The Day of the Scorpion* or consult sociologists of family life before going on to the second sentence of *Anna Karenina*.

The main problem with these views is that we *do* sometimes care whether fictional works tell us true things about the world that we actually live in, not just in some possible world whose relation to our own is unspecified. If we don't usually consult maps or Gallup Polls, we do sometimes attempt to verify statements in fiction in terms of our own real-world experiences. As we read works of literature, we use the specific sentences we find in them as an occasion to think about the real world and experience of it. Based on those sentences, we sometimes formulate our own sentences: "Life for Indians under the Raj was difficult and often humiliating," for instance. As we shall see in Chapter 6, interpretation of this sort plays a major role in the experience of artworks.

Favorable and unfavorable criticism of authors and their creations often depend upon what we believe is true. This is why the following remark on the back cover of *The Day of the Scorpion* is an advertisement for it: "I can't think of anything worth knowing about the Raj in India that Scott hasn't told me. . . . His contribution to literature is permanent." (Excerpt from the *New York Times* review.) Dickens's awareness of the plight of the working classes in the real-life Britain of his times was, with important consequences for social and legal reforms, communicated by many of his novels. Tolstoy perceptively depicts real human relationships. We are interested in whether what is said and implied by his novels is true or false. As Morris Weitz puts it, "Most literary works contain . . . printed or suggested truth claims which we are called upon to take as serious commentaries on life."[27] It is hard to see how we could value literature if it did not include or imply the truth.

Truth in Visual Art

People often claim that truth can also be found in the visual arts. Raphael's painting *Dispute* is alleged to say that the Eucharist is the way to heaven, and placed as it is across the room from the *School of Athens*, it tells us that there are two forms of knowledge: reason and truth. In his collection *American Pictures*, the Danish photographer Jacob Holdt castigates social conditions in the United States in our century as clearly as Dickens's novels portrayed social conditions in the nineteenth century. But if, as some people insist, painting lacks a linguistic structure, how can it make any claims? And how can we say, for example, that a photograph is true or false?

In our culture we find an unmistakable connection between pictures and truth. When we say, for example, that a picture is worth a thousand words, we are saying that a picture *tells* us more than lengthy paragraphs about the same thing are able to do. We often hear paintings described as 'true' or 'false'.

Rembrandt is said to give us a true picture of the psychological character of his subjects. We praise Vermeer for showing us how Delft really looked in the middle of the seventeenth century. George Inness can be accused of lying when he painted a railroad train and track in his 1855 view of the Susquehanna river valley.

Some philosophers insist that only sentences can be true or false. But if pictures are not linguistic, if they contain no sentences (they cannot if they lack vocabulary, syntax, and semantics), then how can pictures convey information? If only sentences can be true, how can we learn anything from something that does not contain any sentences?

We have seen that some pictures are linguistic and can be read as sentences. Hobo signs are ideograms in a primitive language of sorts, and road signs can tell us about road conditions. One test of whether we have a statement is to see if it can be used to lie. Both hobo signs and road signs qualify on this count. They can be used to give us false information. In order to understand these pictures, one must learn a code. Witness Americans' difficulty with understanding signs that are supposed to be visually obvious. Very few people who have not learned the code will see that ▢ means that we are allowed to put clothes in a dryer; or that ⬠ indicates that we should instead hang them on a line.

But the visual artworks with which aesthetics is concerned are not like these examples. Such works of art lack the conventional associations that qualify them even as statements in a code or simple language. Certainly within pictures a halo can signify Christ, a dog can show loyalty, and a bunch of arrows can indicate St. Sebastian. But many paintings do not make straightforward claims of truth. (Consider contemporary abstract art, for instance.) That is, they do not work the way sentences do.

Nonetheless, we do sometimes want to say that paintings are true or false. One way to explain our feeling that some pictures are true, despite the fact that they are not sentences, is to posit a relation of cause and effect between them and the world. The most obvious candidate for this sort of examination is photographs. When we say, "The camera doesn't lie," we are not claiming that photographs are statements but that they are substitutes for the world. The way the world is has direct causal effect on the way photographs turn out. This has led Kendall Walton, for example, to say that photographs are "transparent," that they provide us with a way of seeing the world.[28] A photograph enables me to see how my great grandparents looked in 1890 or how Paris looks in the spring. The way the world looked in 1890 or in Paris in April *caused* the pictures I have seen to appear as they do, and they give me a *true* view.

However, even photographs sometimes "lie." Pornographic photographs of women do not show what women in general want. Lights and shadows in the Yosemite Valley will not appear to the naked human eye in the way they were recorded by Ansel Adams's cameras and films. In a very interesting book about the photography of Edward S. Curtis, Christopher M. Lyman shows how deceptive that photographer's pictures can be.[29] Curtis set out at the beginning of this century to capture what he, and others, feared was a vanishing race of North American Indians. He wanted to preserve "real" Indians as he conceived them—and if the photographs as they turned out did not agree with his conception, he changed them. For instance, when a clock showed up in a tepee, he erased it with an airbrush. We know that he doctored his photographs because we also have undoctored photos taken by him. So some pictures, at least, do seem to provide us with a way of getting at the world. We trust photographs when we have reason to believe that the photographer was not trying to put something over on us. The mere fact that machines (cameras) are used in what is produced does not supply adequate ground for such trust.

On the other hand, the fact that they do not use such machines does not automatically imply that painters and what they create cannot be trusted. We may have as good reason to trust a court reporter's drawing of a witness as a photograph of the same person. We may also have reason to believe that an artist has given us a direct report on how the world looked when we look at a landscape. We may believe that the artist did not intend to deceive us and that the picture we have before us represents correctly what is being depicted. We still do not have a *description* of the world, and this is what distinguishes paintings and statements. A picture is a depiction or presentation of the world that one may use to make statements.

Just as individual sentences in a literary work sometimes serve to suggest claims to readers, so viewers may use a work of visual art as a basis for drawing conclusions about the world. The viewer must provide a sentence that goes with the picture. No picture taken alone can say, "Indians always wore headdresses" or "Women enjoy being humiliated." A picture may be used in a context that leads the viewer to form such a belief, but then the viewer provides the words.

We can use pictures to do all sorts of things that we normally do by means of sentences.[30] I can warn you by saying, "That man has measles" or by drawing a face with a lot of spots on it. The difference is that in the latter case you must, literally, fill in the words. Otherwise, the action misfires.

When we say, then, that works of visual art are true or false, we are being metaphorical or imprecise. Paintings are indirectly true or false. The sentences that viewers subsequently articulate are the literal or direct carriers of truth or falsity.

Truth in Music

Discussions of paintings and literary works are full of statements about what they "say." This is less true of music. However, sometimes claims are made about what a composition *says*—about an idea that it expresses. Brahms's *German* Requiem says, "Death is sad." (This is a drastic oversimplification.) The music accompanying the words has been described as correctly matching the emotion we feel when we realize that "the flower has fallen" (words sung in one of the choruses). More often, and particularly in this century, music has been exclusively subjected to formal or technical analysis—a description of rhythmic and tonal structure.

Indeed, many people maintain that music is *the* one and only purely formal art form, that is, the only art form in which only formal properties are aesthetically relevant. Some theorists believe that to describe music in "literary" ways—to attribute descriptions of rivers to it or even to ascribe emotional expression to it—distorts music. For example, Roger Scruton, a philosopher who is also an accomplished musician, admits that some composers do intentionally try to tell stories or refer to things and events through their work. But this is not the norm, he argues, and even in cases where a composer was trying to say something specific, hearers do not have to listen to the composition in that way. People can understand a piece of music even if they do not know that it is supposed to stand for Melisande's frailty or the flow of the Moldau river, he says.[31]

Some people, however, do think music should be discussed in terms of the statements that it makes, as well as in terms of the emotions that it expresses. We have already seen this idea in the view of Suzanne Langer. The musicologist Susan McClary believes that, in general, it is a mistake to treat music as if it were a "pure" entity isolated from other aspects of cultural and social experience. For example, she interprets Bach's Fifth *Brandenberg* Concerto as an assertion about the growth of individualism in the eighteenth century and a description of the resulting tensions between individual and social interests.[32]

Peter Kivy, another philosopher who is also an accomplished musician, grants that there is no musical semantics in Western music of the sort that would provide dictionary definitions for musical elements.[33] Nonetheless, he believes that music can be treated with more than a strict technical analysis—that it does say or express things. He is primarily interested in the music's capacities for conveying expressions of emotion (and here we see a connection with problems raised in Chapter 2). Kivy thinks that most people's experience of music does make them want to say that some works are "true" or "correct" expressions of joy or grief, for instance.

One mistake that has often been made—and exacerbated by taking the metaphor "language of art" too seriously—is believing that *communication* does not and cannot take place except through the vehicle of language. This mistake, which I believe amounts to a fallacy, is committed more and more often in our "age of information" where terms such as *message, communication, information, speak,* and *think* are used with increasing looseness. For example, Jan L. Broechx says, "If it is true (as psychologically oriented art-critics think) that art contains a certain kind of stimuli to which man reacts as to information, this means *that the work of art is received in the way of messages,* and then the information theory may provide insights into the *development of meanings* in the reception of works of art" (Broechx's italics).[34] But we can react to stimuli that give us information or from which we can extract information without the stimuli necessarily being linguistic in nature. Broechx's use of "messages" here is simply misleading: Either it is incorrect or the term has been so diluted as to render it useless. Surely we obtain information from states of affairs in the world (I see that grass is green) without that state being a message; the world is not a language.

Kivy emphasizes this difference; we can *recognize* emotions in music just as we can recognize them in faces, without our requiring a dictionary or translation manual for features of either musical compositions or faces. We saw earlier that some philosophers disagree with Goodman's conventional theory of representation on the ground that recognition cannot be equated with reading. Kivy believes that the same distinction operates here. When we say that a piece of music is sad, we do not *read* that it is sad, but hear it "as appropriate to expressing" sadness.[35] As Kivy notes, "The opening of the *Lamento d'Arianna* is a perfect icon in sound of the fall of the human voice when it expresses sadness in declaiming 'Let me die!', or something of the kind, just as . . . the opening of the well-known air from *Messiah*, 'Rejoice Greatly, O Daughter of Zion!' resembles the voice rising in joy."[36]

The point is that these are *icons*—signs that resemble what they stand for, not vocabulary items systematically associated conventionally with their references. Signs—what Kivy calls "public criteria of expression"—point to joy and sadness in music just as they do in faces.[37] In both cases the public criteria are literally perceived, read only figuratively.

"Public criteria of expression" contain aspects of both natural and non-natural meaning. We supply the words and provide the sentence, but we do not do so wholly arbitrarily. There may even be connections between the stimuli and responses of the sort Broechx is interested in—for example, typical human responses to certain colors or ascending notes of a major scale. Communication can occur both linguistically and non-linguistically.

Our ascription of an idea to something and our attribution of truth to it require a linguistic system. In both painting and music we fill in the words, specifying what we believe the non-linguistic entity is communicating. We do not *translate* the painting or sonata into English, for translation takes place only between languages. Rather, we *articulate* the meaning.

The particular way in which we articulate an artwork's message depends upon our background. Our experience within our own culture determines how we read—both literally and metaphorically. Emphasis of this point leads us from what some may construe as the narrow question of how or whether works of art function linguistically to broader questions of how art functions in human society and culture. Thus in the next chapter we shall turn to the broader question of art in context.

As we have seen, philosophers disagree about whether works of literature, consisting of sentences within already existing languages, can be true or false. The same question arises with respect to non-literary arts such as painting and music. Though there are difficulties with specifying vocabulary and semantics, these art forms do communicate ideas that are described as being true and false. Readers, listeners, and lookers often articulate claims about the world that are suggested to them by artworks. Confirming or disproving these claims leads to attributing 'truth' or 'falsity' to the works.

NOTES

1. Cesare Ripe, *Iconologica* c. 1600. For an English translation, see Edward Masser's edition (New York: Dover, 1971).

2. Deryck Cooke, *The Language of Music* (Oxford: Oxford University Press, 1959).

3. Nelson Goodman, *Languages of Art* (Indianapolis: Bobbs-Merrill, 1968). See especially Chapter 1.

4. E. H. Gombrich, *Art and Illusion* (New York: Pantheon Books, Random House, 1960). Gombrich's remarks are not always consistent; people have debated what his *real* views are. I shall give my own interpretation. Readers are urged to make their own. Though sometimes inconsistent, Gombrich is one of the most interesting art historians.

5. Ibid., p. 87.

6. H. P. Grice, "Meaning," *Philosophical Review* 66 (1957): 377–88.

7. Charles Sanders Peirce, *The Collected Papers of Charles Sanders Peirce*, ed. Charles Hartshorne and Paul Weiss (Cambridge, Mass.: Harvard University Press, 1960), 2.247, 2.248, and 2.307; pp. 143, 172.

8. 'Icon', as it is being used here, does not refer to the sort of painting often found in churches, as in Russian icons.

9. Erwin Panofsky, *Studies in Iconology; Humanistic Themes in the Art of the Renaissance* (New York: Oxford University Press, 1962; first published 1939).

10. There has been extensive debate on the question of *where* music is—in the score, in the performance, or in the hearing. See, for example, William Webster, "Music Is Not a Notational System," *Journal of Aesthetics and Art Criticism* 29 (Summer 1971): 489–97; and V. A. Howard, "Music and Constant Comment," *Erkenntnis* 12 (January 1978): 73–82.

11. E. H. Gombrich, *The Sense of Order* (Ithaca, N.Y.: Cornell University Press, 1979), p. 210.

12. E. H. Gombrich, "Meditations on a Hobby Horse," in *Meditations on a Hobby Horse* (London: Phaidon Press, 1963).

13. Goodman, *Languages of Art*, pp. 14–15.

14. Goodman has said that he has been badly misunderstood. In a letter to Gombrich he writes, "As you know, I do not hold some of the views often attributed to me. I do not say that representation is entirely a matter of convention, but rather hold that no firm line can be drawn between what is conventional and what is not. This is emphasized in my *Ways of Worldmaking*; and you write that 'the traditional opposition between nature and convention turns out to be misleading.' Bravo! Also I do not deny that realism of representation has something to do with resemblance, but only urge that each affects the other, and that neither goes by unique or absolute standards." Quoted in E. H. Gombrich, *The Image and the Eye* (Ithaca, N.Y.: Cornell University Press, 1982), p. 284. The more extreme view that I have presented—that representation is a matter of convention—is the view that has been repeatedly read from *Languages of Art*. Because the debate has centered about this strong form of the position, it is the one discussed here.

15. Patrick Maynard, "Depiction, Vision, and Convention," *American Philosophical Quarterly* 9 (1972): 248.

16. Richard Wollheim, *Art and Its Objects* (New York: Harper & Row, 1968), pp. 11–18.

17. Roger Scruton, *Art and Imagination* (London: Methuen, 1979), p. 195.

18. Goodman, *Languages of Art*, pp. 127–73.

19. Goodman, *Languages of Art*. Goodman states five requirements for a notational system, two syntactic and three semantic: (1) Syntactic disjointness: "Two marks are character-indifferent if each is an inscription (i.e., belongs to some character) and neither one belongs to any character the other does not" (p. 132). (2) Syntactic finite differentiation: "For every two characters K and K' and every mark m that does not actually belong to both, determination either that m does not belong to K or that m does not belong to K' is theoretically possible" (pp.135–136). (3) Unambiguity: "Characters and inscriptions must have unambiguous compliance-classes" (pp. 148–149). (4) Semantic disjointness: "No two characters have any compliant in common" (p. 151). (5) Semantic finite differentiation: "For every two characters K and K' such that their compliance-classes are not identical, and every object h that does not comply with both, determination either that h does not comply with K or that h does not comply with K' must be theoretically possible" (p. 152).

20. Suzanne Langer, *Feeling and Form* (New York: Scribner's, 1953), p. 31.

21. Gombrich, *A Sense of Order*, p. 102.

22. For examples of this group, see Bertrand Russell, "On Denoting," *Mind* 14 (1905): 479-93; William Sellars, "Presupposing," *Philosophical Review* 63 (1954): 197-215; Willard Quine, *Methods of Logic* (New York: Holt, Rinehart and Winston, 1950), 200-202; A. J. Ayer, *Language, Truth, and Logic* (London: Gollantz, 1946), 44-45; and G. E. Moore, "Symposium on Imaginary Objects," *Proceedings of the Aristotelian Society* suppl. vol. 12 (1933): 55-70.

23. For examples of this group, see P. F. Strawson, "On Referring," *Mind* 59 (1950): 320-44; H.L.A. Hart, "A Logician's Fairy Tale," *Philosophical Review* 60 (1951): 198-212; Gilbert Ryle, "Symposium on Imaginary Objects," *Proceedings of the Aristotelian Society* suppl. vol. 12 (1933): 18-43; and I. A. Richards, *Science and Poetry* (London: Routledge & Kegan Paul, 1935).

24. See, for example, Kendall Walton, "How Remote Are Fictional Worlds from the Real World?", *Journal of Aesthetics and Art Criticism* 37 (1978): 11-24; Nicholas Wolterstorff, "Worlds of Works of Art," *Journal of Aesthetics and Art Criticism* 35 (1976): 120-32; and Robert Howell, "Fictional Objects: How They Are and How They Aren't," *Poetics* 8 (1979): 131-45.

25. For examples, see Arnold Isenberg, "The Esthetic Function of Language," *Journal of Philosophy* 66 (1949): 5-20; Margaret Macdonald and Michael Scriven, "The Language of Fiction," *Proceedings of the Aristotelian Society* 27 (1954): 165-84; and Joseph Margolis, *The Language of Art* (Detroit: Wayne State University Press, 1965), ch. 2.

26. Paul Scott, *The Day of the Scorpion* (London: Granada Publishing, 1968).

27. Morris Weitz, "Truth in Literature," *Revue Internationale de Philosophic* 9 (1955): 116-29.

28. Kendall Walton, "Transparent Pictures: On the Nature of Photographic Realism," *Critical Inquiry* 11 no. 2 (December 1984): 246-77.

29. Christopher M. Lyman, *The Vanishing Race* (New York: Pantheon Books, 1982).

30. Søren Kjørup, "George Inness and 'The Battle of Hastings': Doing Things with Pictures," *Monist* 58 (1974): 216-35.

31. Scruton, *Art and Imagination*, p. 210.

32. Susan McClary, "The Blasphemy of Talking Politics During Bach Year," forthcoming.

33. Peter Kivy, *The Corded Shell* (Princeton, N.J.: Princeton University Press, 1980).

34. Jan L. Broechx, "Aesthetics of Music and Information Theory," in *Contemporary Views of Musical Style and Aesthetics* (Antwerp: Metropolis, 1979), p. 107.

35. Kivy, *The Corded Shell*, p. 50.

36. Ibid., p. 51.

37. Ibid., p. 67.

CHAPTER 5

Aesthetic and Artistic Objects and Their Contexts

> Collins had exposed the fallacy of modern aesthetics to me: . . . "the whole argument from Significant Form stands or falls by volume. If you allow Cezanne to represent a third dimension on his two-dimensional canvas, then you must allow Landseer his gleam of loyalty in the spaniel's eye". . . But it was not until Sebastian, idly turning the page of Clive Bell's Art read: "Does anyone feel the same kind of emotion for a butterfly or a flower that he feels for a cathedral or a picture?" "Yes, I do," that my eyes were opened.
>
> Charles Ryder, *Brideshead Revisited*, by Evelyn Waugh ▮

Our century has witnessed an intense debate among people who have thought that there are proper and improper ways to talk about artistic and aesthetic objects and events. This "form versus content debate" has been broadened recently and might now be described as the "form-context debate." Both sides have had many adherents, though the contentists or contextualists seem to be gaining the majority currently. Collins, referred to in the quotation above, is on this side. Landseer was a popular nineteenth-century British animal painter whose rather moralistic, often sentimental works were favorites of Queen Victoria. Formalist critics spurned his work, arguing that art should be valued because of the *way* it presents things, not because of *what* it depicts. Collins's point is that content is never irrelevant. (The thrust of Sebastian's remark will become clear later.) In this chapter we shall look at this debate and theorists from both camps.

First, however, it is helpful to reflect upon a philosophical issue that shapes the way theorists approach the form-content debate. The argument about whether a work of art must be experienced as an object in and of itself, or can only be appreciated when viewed in a broad context, is related to another question: What kind of thing is a work of art? This is a question about the ontological status of a work of art.

THE ONTOLOGICAL STATUS OF WORKS OF ART

Chapter 4 referred to imitation theories of art, which maintain that works of art are *copies* of reality. They imitate or represent things and events. A movie such as *High Noon* is not "real," we might say—the sheriff and the town never really existed. The film and the real world are not the same. Nonetheless, some people have responded that imitation theories of art overlook the point that artworks have a special kind of reality of their own. If there never was that sheriff, the film is nonetheless *real*.

In sorting out the kind of being that works of art have, philosophers have used several different distinctions. One is that between spatial art forms (those that exist in space—paintings, for example) and temporal art forms (those that exist in time—music, for example). Another is a distinction based upon differences between the performing and the non-performing arts. Philosophers have also applied a distinction used in the philosophy of language, the type-token distinction, to try to explain differences between art forms. Consider the word *dog* in the sentence "John has a dog and Mary has a dog." The word *dog* appears two *different* times, but those two occurrences are instances of the *same* word. Philosophers say that what we have here are two *tokens* of the same *type*. Some art forms exist as types, others as tokens. In literature there are many copies (tokens) of *Hamlet* (type). Several movie theaters can have tokens of the same type. If my copy of *Gone with the Wind* (book or videotape) burns, I can always get another. Kate Smith and José Feliciano may perform it quite differently, but both have sung the same national anthem to open sporting events. But in other art forms there seem to be only types. There is only one *The Way You Hear It Is the Way You Sing It* and only one Empire State Building. If Steen's painting or the Empire State Building is destroyed, we can never experience it again.

The problem of describing the kind of reality works of art have is known as the problem of the ontological status of works of art. What kinds of things are they? Are they physical objects (the particular piece of painted canvas in the Louvre), classes of physical objects (all the copies of *Gone with the Wind*) or not physical at all, but mental or abstract? What and where is the *it* that both Kate Smith and José Feliciano sing? If, as some theories we've seen have argued, a work of art must be viewed in its context, is the context *part* of the work? If not, where does the artwork stop and its context begin?

Some works of art do seem to consist of an object that has a single physical location—paintings and statues, for example. The Mona Lisa is the object currently in a particular spot in the Louvre. Others, though not uniquely locatable, appear to have a tangible reality—physical marks on a page. *Gone with the Wind* or the "Star-Spangled Banner" could be thought of as a class of all their copies. But the latter raises a problem shared by all the performing arts. Is a piece of music, a dance, or a play to be identified with marks on a page or sounds in the air or movements on a stage? If music is sounds, what happens if a composer's work is never performed? Does it exist?

Even those art forms such as painting that can be identified with a particular physical object are puzzling. The Mona Lisa is not exactly the same as it was on the day that Leonardo da Vinci finished painting it. It has aged and has been restored and retouched by others' hands. What reasons, if any, do we have for saying it is the *same* painting?

Several different answers have been given to these questions. Some thinkers who believe that artworks are most dependent on artists for their existence have maintained that the *real* art object exists in the artist's mind. Marks on a page or canvas are only copies of the idea; the *idea* is the real thing, said Benedetto Croce.[1] Other writers believe that the physical embodiment is the artwork. The stone or canvas or sounds or movements constitute the work.[2] After all, without physical embodiments, they maintain, there could be no experience of artworks.

Others have argued that a work of art is not identical with some physical object, but resides in the experience of a physical object. A statue is not just a stone, but "emerges" from it when experienced aesthetically, says Joseph Margolis.[3] David Pole believes that an even more complex account is required to explain the kind of reality that artworks have. He compares them to theories—abstract but public objects and events whose history becomes a part of them.[4] Pole's view of the role of a work's context implies that the very being of a work of art involves that context. If a part of a work is its history, then we cannot understand the work without examining both the thing and its context. If its history becomes part of the object, then context can never be put aside.

I believe that Pole is right to insist that context is crucial—and the theory of art that I present later in this chapter will highlight context. But for several decades earlier in this century such a view would have seemed heretical, and we shall now look at the theory that, for a while at least, dominated art criticism and theory.

FORMALISM

In earlier chapters, we have repeatedly come across what are referred to as "formal properties"—properties such as color, shape, pitch, rhythm, rhyme, and camera angles. Typically such features are distinguished from non-formal properties—properties not located in an object or event, such as the city in which the artwork was created, or the intentions of the artists who made it, or its current owner. Formalism is the view that such properties are exclusively important in aesthetic experience and assessment.

It is important to understand that formalism itself arose largely as a negative response to certain kinds of criticism and as a defense of modern abstract art. One of the heroes of the movement was Cezanne—hence Collins's reference to him in the quotation from *Brideshead Revisited*. To the contemporary eye, Cezanne's paintings do not look very abstract. We can, after all, recognize apples and tables in them as easily as we can recognize people and bagpipes in Steen's painting. But the work was revolutionary and highly criticized in some quarters for not picturing the world the way it really looks. The perspective is often wrong; for example, you cannot tell where in a painting's space some of the things are really supposed to be. In Figure 4 it is hard to see exactly where the edge of the table is located. The apple on the top of the pile is precariously perched, and the bottle in the back seems to float above the table's surface.

Such criticism, when used to try to show that Cezanne was a bad painter, seemed incredibly wrong-headed to this artist's admirers. It showed a misunderstanding of the art of painting, they believed; it confused painting with storytelling. Paintings, the formalists urged, should not be construed as telling us stories about the world. They are not meant to make us think, for example, about apples. Rather they should be construed as telling us, for example, about colors and space. Most recent versions of formalism have insisted that paintings of apples are meant to make us think about *paintings* of apples rather than apples themselves.

Formalist theory and criticism have by no means been limited to the visual arts. Formalist literary critics insist that in literature the text is all-important; the particular words of the text and the way they are put together matter, not what they talk about. In music, it is not the feelings or images evoked that count, but analysis of pitch and rhythm. In all art forms, formalists emphasize intrinsic properties of the object or event itself, not what it represents or expresses. When we look at a work of art, we should not attend to *what it represents* but to *how it presents*. What matters is form, not content—hence the label "formalism."

The two most important figures in formalism for the visual arts (and their influence spread quickly to the other arts) were Clive Bell and Roger Fry. They believed that what matters aesthetically cannot be the content of a work of art, for two works with the same content can be aesthetically very different. Two canvases may both represent people seated around a table, but may not be at all

Figure 4 Cézanne, Still Life: Collection Stedelijk Museum-Amsterdam. Used by permission.

similar aesthetically. One may be balanced, the other unstable. One may be flowing, the other stagnant. One may have delicate colors, the other gaudy ones. Think about two films—a 1940s original and a 1980s remake of it. Obviously they can be very different aesthetically even if the content remains the same. Two works with the same form, on the other hand, will not differ aesthetically.

Form is what is directly presented to and perceived by us. Someone who looks correctly at Steen's *The Way You Hear It* (see Figure 3) will block all of the irrelevant associations that the objects depicted fortuitously have and concentrate on the form alone. Each art form, of course, has its own particular formal qualities. Colors, shapes, and lines are what is special about painting. For music, it is pitches, rhythms, dynamics; for literature, it is syntax, rhythms, images. For dance, it is bodily movements; for film, camera angles or lighting. Fry says that "if imitation [were] the whole purpose of the graphic arts, it [would be] surprising that the works of such arts are ever looked upon as more than curiosities, or ingenious toys, are ever taken seriously by grown up people."[5] He locates the value of art in "the emotions of imaginative life" aroused by perception of purposeful order resulting from the arrangement of the rhythm of lines, mass, space, light and shade, and color.[6]

Clive Bell also bases his aesthetic on the peculiar kind of emotion evoked by art—and by what is peculiar to art: the relations and combinations of lines and colors. He calls this "significant form" and argues that this quality alone evokes the proper sort of response (the special aesthetic emotion referred to in Chapter 3):

> To appreciate a work of art we need bring with us nothing from life, no knowledge of its ideas and affairs, no famil- iarity with its emotions. Art transports us from the world of man's activity to a world of aesthetic exaltation. For a moment we are shut off from human interests; our anticipa- tions and memories are arrested; we are lifted above the stream of life.[7]

Fry also rejects a work's history and context and insists that aesthetic experi- ence has only form as its object:

> Now I venture to say that no one who has a real understand- ing of the art of painting attaches any importance to what we call the subject of a picture—what is represented. To one who feels the language of pictorial form all depends upon *how* it is presented, nothing on what. Rembrandt expressed his profoundest feelings just as well when he painted a carcass hanging up in a butcher's shop as when he painted the Crucifixion or his mistress. Cezanne who most of us believe to be the greatest artist of modern times expressed some of his grandest conceptions in pictures of fruit and crockery on a common kitchen table.[8]

The motivation of formalists then is the desire to identify those special elements that uniquely contribute to the aesthetic nature and appeal of artworks and other objects when they are viewed aesthetically. People are much more likely to describe what is special about the aesthetic, they believe, if they talk about the rhythmic flow of lines in *The Way You Hear It* than if they talk about people sitting around a table. The latter talk tells us nothing about what makes Steen's work succeed as a painting. Someone who thinks primarily about apples will miss what Cezanne is telling us about space, they fear.

Bell and Fry and their followers feel that talk about content or subject matter is talk not about something in the work of art but about something in the world. Our interest in people and apples (at least typically) is not aesthetic; thus we should stop talking about people and apples and start talking about lines and color. As with the aesthetic attitude theorists that we looked at in Chapter 3, formalists are worried that we will be distracted by irrelevant factors when we view artworks, and their remedy is to block out the representational, contentual considerations. They warn people not to be distracted by the "literary element" in art. As one formalist observed, "A painting . . . must live by the strength of the paint alone, must rely on the means which are proper to it, without the aid of melodrama or anecdote."9 For, of course, the melodramatic usually comes from the representational content, not the presentational form. Each of the arts has an analogue. Literature itself must not be looked at in terms of this "literary" element because it is not what is said (the story) but how it is said (the words themselves) that matters.

Critics of formalism usually agree that perceptual qualities of objects are aesthetically important, but insist that content and context matter as well. They believe that what is represented (the representational) is as important as how the materials are presented (the presentational). For example, D. W. Gotshalk writes:

> Artists may use the . . . principles of design . . . on two levels: the presentational and the representational. In a painting there may be harmony or balance between suggested actions or attitudes or between represented personages within a scene or between the glint in the eye and the gesture of an arm of a single represented personage. The representational side of the painting may be as composed, as harmonized, as balanced, as are the lines or shapes or colors. . . . Every overall design, simple or complex, is as individual and unique as the work of art possessing it. To reproduce the design of a picture by Tintoretto, one would have to *copy* the shapes and the lines and colors in the various patterns given them by the painter *and* the personages represented in their dramatic relationships, since these *also* enter into the total structure put there by the artist.10

For Gotshalk, form and content are two different kinds of balance. There is the kind of balance or harmony usually thought of and stressed by the formalists— the proper relation among diagonals, curves, and angles, for instance. But another relationship exists among elements of the subject matter. Just as a sharp angle might be out of place in a painting where lines are primarily flowing, so certain depicted actions or attitudes might be out of place. A sneering Madonna could be inappropriate, for instance. The wrong color used for the parrot in *The Way You Hear It* would upset the balance that now exists between the colors of the bird and the color of the boy's cap, and a bow and arrow in the hands of the woman holding the sheet of music would upset what is now a balance in subject matter. Jerky movements made by the swans would upset the mood of *Swan Lake*, just as harsh consonant sounds would be inappropriate in a gentle love sonnet.

But Gotshalk is saying more than this, and here a serious problem for the formalists arises. He says that in reproducing a painting, one must copy the shapes, lines, color, *and* the attitudes and actions. He writes as if this were not one process, but two. Surely this is absurd. If one copies every line, shape, and color (or movements or words), then the finished product will necessarily be a copy of the "dramatic relationships" as well.

Bell and Fry also talk as if form and content are separable—as if we could look at one and not the other. Gotshalk's remarks only make the impossibility of this patently clear. Statements concerning the representational balance and statements about the presentational balance, of course, constitute different descriptions. But such statements are nonetheless different descriptions of the same thing, not descriptions of two different things.

Try to look at Steen's painting without seeing the old woman or the parrot. Even if we grant that form is more important than content in Cezanne's painting, can we really block out the apples? Perhaps we can squint or stand far enough away so that we cannot identify people or pieces of fruit. But then we no longer really see the paintings at all.

Suppose we *could* see form without seeing the content of representational paintings. This still would not prove that only the former matters. Ad hominum arguments such as Fry's (arguments based on the authority or expertise of the speaker) do not establish that formalist descriptions are the only genuinely aesthetic way of talking about things. How do we know that Fry's is the only genuinely aesthetic experience? Even if it were possible to look at Steen's painting and somehow forget that we are looking at a representation of people sitting around a table having a good time, we cannot be sure that we have separated something that is non-aesthetic.

Bell and Fry argue that the emotional response they feel toward works of art is aroused only by artifacts that possess significant form. When he was asked who feels the same emotion for butterflies as for cathedrals, Sebastian's simple "I do" is a devastating criticism not because it denies the importance of formal properties but rather because it exposes the self-assured arrogance and possible idiosyncracy of the question to which it is a response. The fact that Bell and Fry only respond to the formal properties of artworks does not prove that there are not other things that generate real aesthetic experiences for other people.

It still remains possible that a weaker version of formalism is correct. Even if it is not possible to look just at form, and even if some attention to content constitutes a legitimate element of some aesthetic experiences, perhaps some descriptions of objects and events do not address their aesthetic qualities. In Chapter 2 we discussed the intentional fallacy—the view that reference to artists' intentions is irrelevant in aesthetic discussions. One reason that some people believe this really is a *fallacy* is that they view reference to intention (clearly not a formal feature of art) as not relevant to aesthetic analysis and evaluation. Formalism proclaimed a host of such "fallacies."

Some theorists and critics see the intentional fallacy as but one type of what they call the "genetic fallacy." This is the mistake of confusing artworks with their causes. Understanding the cause, they maintain, does not entail understanding the work of art. Typically the fallacy is thought to be perpetuated by undue attention to the revelations of the artist's biography—attention to conscious intent or subconscious compulsion. But the intentional fallacy also lies as a snare, they think, ready to trap anyone who looks away from the work in the direction of the causes that gave rise to it—to the artist's life or social conditions, for instance, or in the direction of a work's emotional effects, which is called the "affective fallacy."[11]

Formalism is then the position that in aesthetic experience the only things we should attend to or discuss are properties in the object or event itself. The view has been very influential. However, not everyone (myself included) is convinced that aesthetic significance derives from these properties exclusively. We shall now look at the other side and see how content and context matter.

CONTEXTUALISM

In spite of the enormous influence of formalism, people have continued to want, and to receive, the sort of information that these theorists decried. Consider the following description of *The Way You Hear It Is the Way You Sing It* from a Mauritshuis Museum catalogue:

> In addition to Leiden, The Hague, and Delft, Jan Steen also lived in Haarlem. He was the pupil there of Adriaen van Ostade and later returned to live in the city between 1660 and 1670. Steen's last years were spent again in Leiden. His ten years in Haarlem undoubtedly constitute the highpoint of his career. Steen showed a taste for monumental compositions in these years. Our painting is one of Steen's masterpieces from this period, but not simply because of its large format; it exhibits an exceptionally clever composition which unites the two halves of the scene through the figure of the youth pouring wine. It is noteworthy that among various Haarlem works a typical Delft school element appears: the brightly lighted white plaster back wall which is so reminiscent of Vermeer's interiors and Fabritius's *Goldfinch*. This painting proves that Steen not only excelled in

cabinet-sized paintings, like the *Girl Eating Oysters*, but also could successfully carry out a large work.

This painting also confirms Steen's reputation as a humorist. Since Steen used members of his own family and himself for models, the canvas came to be known as "Jan Steen's Household." A "Huisholden van Jan Steen" (Jan Steen's Household) is an epithet today in the Netherlands for a lively and untidy home. The painting's title, however, overlooks the work's deeper meaning. The grandmother in the foreground holds a paper in her hand on which an old Dutch rhyme can be read—"So voorgesongen, so nagepepen . . ." (the way you hear it is the way you sing it). Jan Steen thus issues a gentle warning against children's tendency to imitate their parents. In so doing he offers a witty visual play on the different meanings of the word 'pijpen' (pipe or to pipe); Jan Steen, the figure wearing a hat, gives his young son a draft from his *pipe* while behind him a somewhat older youth plays a *bagpipe*. The parrot's famed ability to mimic reemphasizes the letter's adage.[12]

Here the author talks about formal properties (white light or composition) but also about content (children's imitation or pouring wine). Dogged insistence that we ignore the fact that the bagpipes symbolized sexual looseness or the parrot mimicry because it detracts from our aesthetic experience simply flies in the face of most people's enjoyment of artworks.

Thus there has recently been increasing reaction against formalist strictures. Many writers insist upon their right to talk about content. Other people argue that genetic and affective considerations are not fallacies at all, but parts of the complex activity of experiencing, interpreting, and evaluating central to aesthetic contemplation of something. We saw in Chapter 4 that Cooke, Kivy, and McClary argue for due attention to the role of expression and statement in music. All of these writers represent a growing impatience with a narrow formal analysis that seems to bind criticism and distort many individuals' experience of music.

Discussions of art, however, are not even limited to properties of works themselves—whether of form, content, or expression. Notice that in the discussion of Steen's painting just quoted, the writer refers to Steen's life, other Dutch painters and paintings, and Dutch culture. Some theorists have maintained that an understanding of art and the aesthetic demands attention to all of these elements. That is, they insist that understanding the *context* in which an object or event is created and experienced is essential if we are to perceive it correctly. We shall begin considering theories of context by looking at two ways in which history and tradition have figured in explanations of art and the aesthetic.

The Role of Tradition and History

Marxist Aesthetics

Marxist critics and philosophers have never been attracted to formalism. They have been interested in what we can call *aesthetic sociology*—the way art functions socially, politically, economically, and historically. Thus Marxist critics look for patterns and relationships that art has and shares with other social creations, and they evaluate art on the basis of its historical role and its contribution to furthering Marxist social ideals. Practitioners of this type of contextual analysis see themselves as involved in a political movement, not simply as theorists within a particular academic school.

According to Marxist aesthetics, art (like everything else) is produced by historical conditions and so needs to be explained in terms of those conditions, particularly in terms of the ideologies that are reflected in and perpetuated by them. For example, Renaissance sculpture cannot be understood apart from understanding the nature of guilds, nor can contemporary American art be understood apart from the corporate market, Marxists claim. Ideologies shape values and ways of perceiving, so people don't *choose* to view works in a certain way; their view is *determined* for them. This is true both for form and content, although most Marxists are interested primarily in the latter. We must know what Jan Steen's position in his society was (that he was a rich businessman, for instance), what wars the Netherlands were engaged in, what new developments there were in the shipping trade, and otherwise understand his world if we are to adequately understand his painting. We must also grasp the deeper epistemological and metaphysical ideology that pervaded Steen's class and period—that is, we must know what people's attitudes toward and theories about reality, knowledge, and truth were during the period.

One of the most fascinating Marxist studies is John Berger's analysis of the development and popularity of the genre of oil painting. Although formalists certainly stress the importance of the medium of a particular work—whether it is done in oils, watercolor, or charcoal, for example—they do so because the medium is supposed to be an intrinsic perceptual feature whose relevance we can grasp directly. Berger believes this is wrong. Instead, he thinks the medium chosen is important because it reveals essential facts about society and vice versa. The predominant use of oils arose when "there was a need to develop and perfect this technique . . . in order to express a particular view of life for which the techniques of tempera or fresco were inadequate."[13] According to Berger, "What distinguishes oil painting from any other form of painting is its special ability to render the tangibility, the texture, and solidity of what it depicts. It defines the real as that which you can put your hands on."[14] Oil paintings are commodities that depict commodities, possessions that depict possessions. Consider the paintings that we see on the walls of castles and manor houses; they are part of the furniture, part of the owner's worldly goods. The obviously corporeal, full-bodied quality of oil expresses this well. Different cultures wih different senses of reality will have different art. In a society with a more abstract, non-materialist worldview, oil painting will be unlikely to play much of a role, Berger suggests. The fact that ink is a more popular medium in Eastern art is very significant.

Walter Benjamin provides another example of the way in which the character of a culture mirrors and is mirrored by the kinds of artworks produced in it. He has described the ways in which he believes modern techniques that allow for mass reproduction and appeal, especially film, are undermining the capitalistic perception of art as constituted by a few masterpieces.[15] Musical videos are having a rapid and pronounced affect on musical art forms. It will be fascinating to see whether highly trained (elite) individuals are replaced by machines as has been predicted and whether this causes music to play a different role in the lives of the masses.

Marxists who believe that art, like everything else, is governed by economic institutions and motives, are often, but not always, critical of non-leftist art. The best of them go beyond discussions of works of art mainly in terms of the economic or political structures the artworks reflect. They do not see criticism primarily as a means of calling for reactions against fascist formalism in favor of the working class. Terry Eagleton, for example, has a broader agenda.

> To write well is more than a matter of "style"; it also means having at one's disposal an ideological perspective which can permeate to the realities of men's experience in a certain situation. . . . This is certainly what the Placido Gulf scene (in Conrad's *Nostromo*) does; and it can do it, not just because its author happens to have an excellent prose-style, but because his historical situation allows his access to such insights. Whether these insights are in political terms "progressive" or "reactionary" (Conrad's certainly are the latter) is not the point—any more than it is the point that most of the agreed major writers of the twentieth century—Yeats, Pound, Lawrence—are political conservatives who each had truck with fascism. Marxist criticism, rather than apologising for the fact, explains it—sees that, in the absence of genuinely revolutionary art, only a radical conservatism, hostile like Marxism to the withered values of liberal bourgeois society, could produce the most significant literature.[16]

One of the problems with Marxism (and other sociologies of art) is that it assumes a connection between art and social features that has yet to be shown to exist. That is, it presupposes the existence of lawlike connections between social factors and artistic creation. There may be connections between, for example, economic life and the prevailing medium of artworks produced, but their existence must be empirically verified. And how are we to account for the exceptions? In Holland while Steen and Vermeer painted capitalistic possessions and leisure activity, Rembrandt continued to paint Biblical scenes. Why?

In many ways, the problems with Marxist aesthetics are the opposite of those I claimed confront formalism. Formalism calls for a narrow isolation of artworks from their contexts and hence distorts them and our experience of them. Marxism identifies artworks with their contexts and hence does not allow us to see what is special about them. There is a sense in which Marxist aesthetics ceases to be aesthetics at all. In calling for a holistic approach to art—and everything else—one begins to lose sight of why we need to concentrate on art in particular. If paintings are created and valued for the same reasons that, say, newspapers or automobiles are created and valued, it is hard to explain what is special about art. If we must know everything about an object's context in order to "get" it, it is easy to become skeptical about ever being able to understand anything. We shall return to this problem later.

Historical and Artistic Categories

Marxist theorists are interested in the very broad ways in which history affects art. The analytic philosopher Kendall Walton is interested in how art history affects our experience of it. In "Categories of Art," he addresses the question of whether reference to extrinsic information is aesthetically important, or whether, as formalists and anti-intentionalists insist, it is intrinsic properties alone that matter aesthetically. Information about *extrinsic properties* tells us things about artworks that cannot be discovered just by looking at the works themselves, such as where they were made or who owns them. Information about *intrinsic properties* tells us what is in the works themselves. He asks whether, for example, critical questions about works of art can be separated from their histories, and he answers that they cannot.

Walton agrees with formalists that aesthetic experience involves attending to intrinsic features of objects. But this attention is selective, he thinks. Not all of an object's intrinsic features are relevant, and determining which ones count demands extrinsic information. Perception of aesthetic features, he says, depends upon which non-aesthetic features are "standard," which "variable," and which "contra-standard."[17] *Standard features* are features that determine which category a work belongs to. Flatness, for example, is a standard feature of painting. *Variable features* have nothing to do with whether a work belongs to a category. A painting's subject matter is a variable feature. *Contra-standard features* are those whose presence tends to disqualify a work as a member of a category. Three-dimensionality is a contra-standard feature of painting. According to Walton, "What aesthetic properties a work seems to have, what aesthetic effect it has on us, how it strikes us aesthetically often depends (in part) on which of its features are standard, which variable, and which contra-standard for us."[18] For example, since flatness is standard for portraits, being flat will not prevent a painting from looking like Queen Elizabeth. Only variable properties, such as the color of paint used for the hair or eyes, will matter.

We must know which features are which before we are in a position to perceive a work correctly. We cannot discover this simply by looking at the work itself as if it were an entity that could be isolated from its history or context, Walton argues. The statements we make about works, including attribution even of formal properties such as rhyme or color, depend upon putting the object in the right category such as sonnet or pastel. And putting artworks into the right category is a complex function of standard features, history, and social practice. Information about all of these is relevant to an understanding of a work.

Art has a history that determines which features are standard, variable, and contra-standard. A poet cannot decide to write an Elizabethan sonnet with only two lines, and we cannot experience a couplet as a sonnet. To have an experience of a *sonnet* we must know what being a sonnet entails. Thus we have to bring external information to our reading to experience the poem correctly and assess its rhythm and rhyme scheme.

According to Walton then, we simply cannot know what a work's aesthetic qualities are just by looking closely or by listening carefully. Appreciation of art demands training and attention that go far beyond immediate perceptual experience.

This idea explains why Collins is right when he says that modern aesthetics—that is, formalism—rests on a mistake. Formalists insist that we only attend to what is there. But attributing volume to Cezanne's apples—that is, to his *flat* surfaces—is as much a matter of reading something into the painting as is finding facial expression (a glint in the spaniel's eye) in the paint or of hearing comments on individualism in the Fifth *Brandenburg* Concerto. If they belong to the proper category (animal painting, for instance), some two-dimensional objects yield a three-dimensional interpretation. Some objects lend themselves to interpretation in terms of an expression of emotion or idea. The formalists' mistake is treating all artworks as if they belong to the same category.

The Role of Institutions

Another very important contextual approach—called the "institutional theory of art"—stresses the role of social practices and institutions. As with Marxism, it is a reaction against formalism and favors regarding art as a social phenomenon. But it is not a self-consciously political movement and is more traditionally philosophical in having as its goal the articulation of a definition of the term 'art'. Institutional theories also arose in response to the sorts of developments in twentieth-century art we encountered in the first chapter—with such movements as "found art," minimalism, happenings, and conceptual art. Boulders in public parks, thrown paint, soup cans, and urinals in museums, cacophonies resulting from frying eggs and chopping up pianos in concert halls, and repetitions of a single word in poetry anthologies created new problems for art theorists. It appeared to an increasingly large audience that there was very little distinguishing works of art from anything else—that art had become whatever anybody said it was.

But such an extreme relativism is unacceptable to some theorists, and we have tried to explain the difference between art and non-art in terms of social practices and institutions that can be identified and distinguished, and which in turn allow for separating off the objects and events with which they are concerned.

Dickie's Institutional Theory of Art

The most widely debated institutional thoery of art is George Dickie's, largely because he provides a clearly stated definition of 'art', which crystalizes features and hence is conducive to focused discussion (a real achievement in itself):

> A work of art in the classificatory sense is (1) an artifact, (2) a set of the aspects of which has had conferred upon it the status of candidate for appreciation by some person or persons acting on behalf of a certain social institution (the artworld).[19]

The restriction to "classificatory sense" is intended to emphasize that most institutionalists see a difference between our using the term 'work of art' to describe (to assign membership in a class) and to evaluate. They insist that they are only interested in what makes something art, not in explaining what makes something good or bad art.

Few have quarreled with Dickie's first requirement that art works must be artifacts. Nearly everyone agrees that works of art must be made by someone. But the second condition has received attention. Dickie believes that although there are no rigid, formalized rules for conferring status, it can be compared to christening or knighting, where there is an obvious sense in which "saying makes it so" but only under certain conditions. The President of the United States, with all the power attached to that office, cannot dub someone a knight. On the other hand, a friend with very limited power can install you as a member of her club *if* a certain set of stipulated rituals has been agreed to in advance. Conventions must, and do, exist in contemporary culture if a bunch of boulders can become a work of art. Dickie writes:

> My thesis is that, in a way analogous to the way in which a person is certified as qualified for office, or two persons

acquire the status of commonlaw marriage within a legal system, or a person is elected president of the Rotary, or a person acquires the status of wise man within a community, so an artifact can acquire the status of candidate for appreciation within the social system called "the artworld." How can one tell when the status has been conferred? An artifact's hanging in an art museum as part of a show and a performance at a theater are sure signs. There is, of course, no guarantee that one can always know whether something is a candidate for appreciation, just as one cannot always tell whether a given person is a knight or married. When an object's status depends upon non-exhibited characteristics a simple look at the object will not necessarily reveal that status. The non-exhibited relation *may* be symbolized by some badge, for example, by a wedding ring, in which a simple look will reveal the status.[20]

Most of the problems with this definition center about the concepts of conferring. One of the best criticisms is by Ted Cohen.[21] He is concerned that the artworld, the conferring agency, is so loose that we will never be able to tell if conferral has been successful. Christenings require established rituals. If becoming a work of art is like being christened, then the burden is on Dickie to state the analogous ceremonies. He has not; and Cohen is dubious about the possibility of so doing.

The problem with 'appreciation' is that Dickie's definition assumes a common or characteristic form of it that qualifies all positive artistic experience. Cohen doubts that such a commonality exists because art forms differ so much from one another. Is our pleasure in a symphony really the same as that in a film? Our response even seems to change within the same genre. We do not enjoy Steen in the same way that we do Cezanne or Van Gogh, let alone as we do contemporary painters like Pollock or Dali. These considerations suggest to Cohen:

> (1) that being a candidate for appreciation in any but the emptiest sense of "appreciation" . . . is not part of what it is to be an artwork, at least not for some works, and (2) that possibilities concerning what *can* be appreciated have some bearing on what can be made a candidate for appreciation. The second point is not considered by Dickie, and this is responsible for what I think of as a formal gap in his definition.[22]

Richard Wollheim believes that the difficulties in institutional theories amount to more than gaps in the definition. He first questions the classification/evaluation distinction that institutionalists make. As we use the term *work of art*, he argues, both features are present. We imply not just that an object belongs to a particular class, but that it is also valuable. Thus a definition that deals only with classification will inevitably be limited at best.

But the crucial question, Wollheim says, is this: "Is it to be presumed that those who confer status upon some artifact do so for good reason, or is there no such presumption?"[23] When the boulders were put on exhibition, was there a good reason for doing so, or was it a whim or an insult or a response to external pressure? Surely if something deserves to be called 'art', someone must be able to justify its being treated that way. If we have an account of what constitutes good reasons, then we shall have an independent basis on which to found a definition of 'art'. But then calling something a work of art amounts not simply to having status conferred upon it, but to having clear, good reasons for conferring the status. Conferring (dubbing) will then be tantamount to confirming or recognizing that the reasons apply in a given case.

Even if confirmation is required in addition to good reasons, the details of what this confirmation consists of are woefully unanalyzed, Wollheim thinks. He also objects that 'appreciation' begs the important questions by concealing the good reasons that might serve independently as a definition: "When Ruskin accused Whistler of flinging a pot of paint in the public's face, he was in effect saying that Whistler could not be putting his paintings forward as candidates for appreciation."[24] If I present an object to you for your appreciation, I must present it for a special kind of appreciation if it is to be treated as a work of art. As soon as we try to specify the kind of appreciation required, we shall find ourselves back where we started.

Danto's Theory of Art in an Artworld

In a series of essays in the early 1960s, Arthur Danto introduced the term 'artworld' to cover the loose group of institutions that he believes are responsible for the fact that in our society some, but not all, objects are identified as artworks. The artworld, as Danto understands it, includes museums, orchestras, theaters, literary magazines, publishers, arts councils, art funding agencies, classrooms, ballet companies, and art dealerships. The artworld gives artworks a special kind of existence. A boulder is a boulder wherever it is found; but only within the artworld can it also be a work of art. Thus Danto has what might be called a metaphysical institutional theory of art, one that takes us back in the history of philosophy of art in order to explain how the kind of reality that artworks have depends upon social institutions. According to the ancient Greeks, especially Plato and Aristotle, art is not real in the same way the world is real. A bed and a picture of a bed are quite different kinds of things; the latter is an imitation of the former. Even if a highly illusionistic picture of a bed fools us for a while, eventually—when we try to lie down on it, for instance—we will discover the difference between the imitation and the real thing.

The imitation theory of art—the theory that all art is an imitation of reality—has been criticized for several reasons. (Some criticisms were discussed in Chapter 4; others were mentioned earlier in this chapter.) Danto thinks that this theory has become particularly vulnerable in our century—when we would not, for example, be surprised to find a real bed (one people could sleep on) in a museum exhibit of contemporary art. As an object, the museum bed does not lack some property that a real bed has, nor does it have some special physical property that a real bed lacks. The artwork is not part of the bed nor vice versa.

Danto believes that when we say something is a work of art, we are using *is* in a special way. The *is* in the predicate "is a work of art" he calls "the 'is' of artistic identification."[25] This special use of *is* needs a theory for its interpretation—one that keeps the museum bed from "collapsing into reality." When we fully understand the sentence, "That bed is a work of art," we see that it says, "That bed is a work of art according to theories of art held in our (or some) artworld." Danto thus requires more in the way of theory than Dickie. For something to be an artwork, the artworld and the artist presenting something for candidacy for appreciation must share a *theory* about what art is.

Because there is a difference between a work of art and the physical body that embodies it, we use different languages to describe the two, and the same physical object might actually embody different artworks, according to Danto.[26] (The same piece of stone might be two different works of sculpture—one entitled, for instance, *Mushroom*, the other *Holocaust*.) Whether we respond to a physical object as a work of art at all, and the way we describe it, depends on the culture to which we belong. As Danto notes, "To see an artwork without knowing it is an artwork is comparable in a way to what one's experience of print is, before one learns to read; and to see it as an artwork then is like going from the realm of mere things to a realm of meaning."[27] (This observation is reminiscent of the writers we looked at in Chapter 4 who believe that reading works of art is like reading language.) According to Danto, the way we "read" an object ontologically depends upon our social theories and institutional practices with regard to art.

Eaton's Theory of Art Within Traditions

As with Danto's view, my own points beyond objects to their context. But in addition to insisting upon the existence of theories, I also, as Walton does, emphasize the role of traditions of art criticism and history. I have been very much influenced by institutionalists and have developed a definition that I believe avoids some of the objections to which Dickie's definition is vulnerable.

If we consider the things that have been called 'art' (even if we consider only the paradigmatic cases—"great art"), it is sooner or later apparent that no directly observable properties separate them from things that have never been called art. Twentieth-century art has only underlined this fact. Furthermore, we saw in

Chapter 1 that Weitz worried that defining 'art' destroys the creative aspects essential to its activity. If we turn from directly observable properties of the objects to our experiences of them, we seem no better off. For, as Sebastian in *Brideshead Revisited* shows us, this will not distinguish butterflies from cathedrals. Considerations such as these have been the source of a great deal of skepticism toward the possibility of ever formulating a definition. P. F. Strawson believes we get bogged down in the "limitless elasticity and variety of the vocabulary of criticism" when we try to define 'art'.[28]

Nonetheless, I think there is something special about artworks, namely, the way we treat them. We do not just point to things and call them 'art'. We protect them, we revere them, we display them. But most especially we *talk* about them. Indeed, protection, reverence, and display are usually strategies for bringing about and enhancing discussion. Thus one approach to understanding the nature of art—and its differences from non-art—is to ask whether there is anything *special* about the way we talk about it. Is a particular vocabulary used? Do we tend to point to one sort of thing or to use one category of information rather than another?

A survey of "talk about art" (in which I include all kinds of talk, from journal articles to letters to the editor, from catalogues of exhibitions to concert program notes) comes up short if what we hope to find is something special in or about the *content*. In attempting to bring about an understanding of works of art, we seem to need all kinds of data; no single fact is necessary or sufficient for artworks. We find facts given about the artist's life (Steen lived in Leiden), interpretation of subject matter (the heroine is turned into a swan), reference to formal qualities (the minor second is repeated throughout and unifies the symphony), and suggestions about consequences (the book changed the public's attitude toward slavery). No one thing is talked about only or always, and the same things are offered in discussions about objects that are not works of art. Anything and everything about what we can call their history of production can be relevant (and this includes consequences as well as causes, whatever tells the "story" of its production). What is special about discussions of art is not their content, but their purpose—not *what* is said, but *why* it is said. Viewers are brought (or intended to be brought) to perceive things that might have been missed had they been left to their own devices. These things are located in the work and are considered capable of giving us pleasure. Thus I propose the following definition of 'art':

> x is a work of art if and only if x is an artifact and x is discussed in such a way that information concerning its history of production brings the audience to attend to intrinsic properties considered worthy of attention in aesthetic traditions (history, criticism, theory).[29]

This definition relies heavily on the notion of 'the aesthetic'. We must turn to aesthetic traditions to identify what all the talk about art is to direct our attention toward. If we cannot at least roughly specify what we mean by 'the aesthetic', then the definition will not advance our understanding of 'work of art' very far. I think that we can describe what aesthetic traditions are, but since my characterization involves the concept of *value*—the definition rests on what is *worthy* of attention—I shall delay this part of the discussion until Chapter 7.

One thing in favor of my definition is that it does not foreclose the possibility of creativity. Artists are not restricted in the properties that they can offer for attention. The definition also allows for the fact that at different times and in different places different things are considered worthy of attention. In literature, plot, then character, then the process of writing itself have dominated discussions. In our own period we are not just witnessing development of the possibilities for mechanical and electronic reproduction but are also revising views about what constitutes the canon of art. "Women's work" such as quilt making is now being discussed in ways that bring us to attend to qualities that are finally being recognized as worthy of serious aesthetic attention.

The definition explains why we keep objects safe: We have to be able to attend to them. It also explains why some things fail to achieve the status of art: They don't get talked about. Boulders may be arranged on a grassy space, marks may be made on paper, but until they are discussed as works of art, they are not yet works of art. Undiscovered pages with markings on them are potentially poems or engravings or symphonies; they do not actually become full-fledged works of art until they are treated and experienced as artworks.

But there is a problem. If the definition is correct, must it not follow that all art is good? Something can be a knife, say, without its being a good knife; it can slice without slicing well. But if something is "worthy of attention" it would seem it must be good.

There has been very little discussion of bad art in the history of art and aesthetics. Artists and critics often try to change our minds about what is generally considered bad—to make us take soap operas or comic books seriously, for example. But there is not much discussion of what people believe to be really bad or unredeemable. Hence understanding of it is very shallow.

Other than denying the existence of bad art, and I am more certain it exists every time I look for a birthday card, one way to save the definition would be to incorporate the concept of taste. We could then limit ourselves to "things considered worthy of attention by people with taste." It does often appear that an elite cadre or "in group" rules the artworld. But we have already seen in Chapter 3 what serious problems there are for taste.

Instead I think we need to talk about "types" or "sorts" of intrinsic properties. Mogen David is bad wine; but it is wine because it has the properties—alcoholic content, fruit base, bouquet, and color—that we associate with wine. Similarly, bad art has shape, color, and expressive qualities—properties considered worthy of attention. But in bad art these things simply do not create a positive response.

Just as we distinguish art from non-art on the basis of properties identified as worthy of attention, so what is good and bad are culturally determined. The properties identified as worthy of attention are historically tied to institutions and practices in our societies. Color or rhyme matter to us; they may not matter in another cultural context. Once they matter, having good or bad colors will depend upon the particular object to which we attend.

All of the institutional theories of art we have discussed insist that outside the context of social and cultural practices and conventions, 'art' does not make sense. Institutions such as museums or critical practices must "dub" things, or theories and traditions must be shared, before art can be distinguished from non-art. The question "Which things are works of art?" cannot be answered, institutionalists claim, until one locates institutions, theories, or traditions that lend status to certain things but not to others.

Another way of dealing with the question "Which things are works of art?" is to respond that the question cannnot be answered—to say that a work's essence can never be fully determined or that a work of art is not one thing but many, that there are as many works as there are individual experiences of it. The object is an occasion of reading or seeing or hearing, not a single thing that is read or seen or heard. This ontological view is at the heart of another contextual approach to art and the aesthetic—one that is quite different from the analytical views that we have examined to this point.

STRUCTURALISM AND DECONSTRUCTION

Two contemporary movements known respectively as structuralism and deconstruction have their origins in continental European philosophy and art theory; they have not been popular with philosophers in the Anglo-American analytic tradition. These movements are important, however, if only because of the negative responses that they have incited—particularly deconstruction, whose supporters and detractors are currently engaged in heated debates. But first, let's look briefly at its predecessor, structuralism.

Structuralists contend that basic myths and stories are found everywhere. Songs, plays, and paintings that depict, for instance, the coming of spring or love/hate relationships between parents and children are found in all cultures. So are such artistic forms as tragedy, comedy, satire, and poetry. Essentially a sociological and anthropological approach to the aesthetic, structuralism regards art as a reflection of other aspects of society and regards societies as exhibiting general laws.

One of the earliest and most important structuralists is the French anthropologist Claude Lévi-Strauss. In one sense, Lévi-Strauss agrees with formalists in emphasizing the form of a work of art. Indeed, for him works of art become akin to formulas. For example, something in a high place is portrayed as encountering something in a low place, and the latter is elevated. (Notice that this can apply to musical works as well as to literary or visual works.) The particular content is made to fit, much in the way that the proper values are replaced for variables in a mathematical formula. Relations have to be preserved, and hence there are rules for putting together the parts of a narrative or the movements in a symphony.

Story-formulas (or "pretexts," as they are often called) and rules for constructing full works from them pervade all cultures, Lévi-Strauss believes. In particular they pervade the objects we set aside for special scrutiny—works of art. Artworks reflect their own structures, but they also reflect those of the cultures in which they are constructed. Art moves us because, as Lévi-Strauss observes, "It arrests in time the dissipation of the contingent in favor of the pretext and incorporates it into the work."[30] (Such writing is typical of structuralists and deconstructionists.)

Critics accuse structuralists of being so concerned with myth-formulas that they read these formulas into everything they come across and thus suffer from a myopia that prevents them from getting at what is most essential about artworks, namely, their uniqueness. They have also been charged with failing to realize that they are seeing with their own eyes only and have no way of proving that the story or myth they think they are discovering was the one put there originally.

Structuralism is an attempt to *reconstruct* the form and content of a work according to general, repeatable social phenomena. An important poststructural movement has called itself *deconstruction*.

Deconstructionists claim that all contextual theories are based on a mistake— the mistake of believing that we have accesss to the contexts necessary for understanding art and aesthetic experience. Deconstructionists believe that the access to contexts upon which such theories rely are not available and hence that they collapse. The reasoning is as follows: It is true that understanding art depends on understanding the circumstances and conditions of its production. However, we cannot attain such understanding. Even works created in our own contemporary culture are beyond our grasp, for we are never in all ways like the creator. Thus we cannot understand works of art, if by "understanding" we mean getting at the single correct interpretation of them.

In some ways it is easiest to grasp the problems that deconstructionists think we face by considering an (apparently) simple example—an everyday statement such as, "John will be at the train station at four o'clock." To understand someone who says this, we must fill in many missing words—words that we assume to be mutually understood when the statement is uttered in a particular situation: John who, which train station, when (morning or afternoon). We must also know a great deal about the speaker and hearer and their relationship. Does the speaker intend the hearer to take her seriously? Does the hearer trust the speaker? Are they actors in play? Is this a request or a warning? Even when someone to whom we are very close—a spouse, sibling, or best friend—says something like this, we cannot be sure that we have completely gotten the message or correctly interpreted the attitude it expresses.

How much more complicated it becomes when we turn to texts produced in times and places removed from our own. The very questions we ask about art are rooted in our own historical period. For example, "Who was the artist?" has not always been considered an important question. If meaning is historic, how can we ever get it? Only one answer, "We can't!", has seemed correct to a number of philosophers and critics. The ensuing skepticism (sometimes accompanied by frustration and despair, sometimes by exhilaration and a sense of being "free at last") has often resulted in a radical relativism both of meaning and interpretation. This position claims that I cannot know what you mean, and thus I can only interpret your words in my own way. My way will necessarily be different from your way, and "correct way" becomes an empty, meaningless concept.

Deconstructionists say that the context always changes a sign's meaning; words, hobo signs, woman-shapes, or notes will mean different things in different sentences, on different fences, in different paintings, and in different scores. Thus meaning is never completely "present." Even in the case of a spoken utterance (which deconstructionists accuse Western philosophy of having wrongly given priority) the meaning is never completely present. What is not said is as crucial as what is said; "absence," they insist, is signified as much or more than "presence" is. Thus deconstructionists attempt to show how important "absence" is. An apparently simple statement is shown to reveal as much by what is not said (what is absent) as from what is said (what is present). Paying attention to absences as well as presences in "John will be at the train station at four o'clock" yields important insights, they think: "Mary will not be at the train station," "John will not be home," or "John is of a lower social class than people who use airports," for instance.

Deconstructionists also try to show what ideological principles are at work in texts and utterances. They have been particularly interested in binary opposites at work in Western conceptual schemes, for example male/female, even/odd, slave/master, either/or. They try to "deconstruct" these pairs to show that they are not ultimately exclusive. For example, the slave/master dichotomy, when deconstructed, shows that dependence is central to both. A slave is obviously dependent on a master, but one cannot be a master without a slave.

In one sense then, deconstruction is a type of interpretation at a very deep level. As viewers we can never reconstruct an artist's meaning, or equate a work with symbols operating in a particular time or place, or understand what a work would mean to most people in a given audience. We can, however, use a work to get at ideologies existing in the culture in which it was produced. A deconstructionist might deconstruct *High Noon*, for instance, by analyzing the western movie as a special film genre. The film would be viewed as revealing a worldview in terms of good and bad, leaders and followers, law abiders and criminals, strong and weak, powerful and powerless. A feminist might deconstruct the film in terms of its portrayal of male and female roles, with duty tied to violence and nurturing tied to non-violence. Such discussions have a very different focus from those in which primary attention is given to the way shots of the clock are used to build up suspense.

But deconstruction is more than just another method of interpretation. Its adherents hope to show that there is more to a symbol or "signifier," as they call it, than meanings conventionally connecting them to the world. At the same time, deconstructionists hope to show that objects identified as "great art" are no more meaningful than other objects. Great artworks are not objects to be revered; they are not things to which we owe an effort whose goal is capturing their essence as fully as possible. Art objects are not removable from their contexts any more than political speeches or TV ads are. Their producers have their feet firmly stuck in the clay of societies permeated by ideologies and significances beyond their control. The smallest details can be the most important—for these will be as likely to convey the principles by and with which an artist worked as will the title or central theme. A frame may be more important than the painting it frames. One of the consequences of such a view is what is described as "opening up the canon." Comic books as well as the plays of Shakespeare, or films starring the Three Stooges as well as grand operas starring Pavarotti, are considered worthy of serious study.

Since we cannot *decide* what the meaning is, a text often becomes an occasion not for interpretation but for playing around with the words, for getting "John will be strained" from "John will be at the train station" for instance. Still the play is often deadly serious, for deconstructionists, like Marxists, regard themselves as much a political as an academic movement. Its founder and most important spokesperson, Jacques Derrida, is particularly concerned about the power that languages have.[31]

One of the difficulties with deconstruction, beyond its typically studied obscurity, is the intentional slipperiness it attaches to the concepts we are accustomed to using in analytic philosophy—vague as those concepts may be. A question such as "What does the poem mean?" is at the same time dismissed and taken very seriously. In one sense, there is no meaning; in another sense, there is an excess of it. As Geoffrey Hartman has written, "Literary language foregrounds language itself as something not reducible to meaning; it opens as well as closes the disparity between symbol and idea, between written sign and assigned meaning."[32] On the one hand, deconstructionists share with Marxists the view that social factors cannot be separated from a work; on the other hand, they are dubious about our ever constructing an adequate interpretation even when these factors are taken into account.

We shall have more to say in the next chapter about the possibility of verifiable interpretations. For now, note that by no means everyone has accepted such relativistic attitudes. A number of critics and theorists believe that we can get at the meaning of a work of art, even if that demands understanding its context. Such writers regard as incorrect the skeptical position, which denies the possibility of locating ourselves within a different context because our feet are stuck in the concrete of our own. Anthony Savile says that such a position "denies the legitimacy of our critical practice while stressing its practical inevitability."[33] As a firm supporter of a brand of contextualism that he calls "historicism," he criticizes the view that it is impossible to resurrect enough of a past context to view a work as it was viewed when it was created. He argues that our own mental set does not always prevent us from understanding work produced by someone else.

Savile believes that "we can ourselves do something by way of selecting or changing those sets."[34] Of course, we cannot completely determine the way we look at something. But we can know, for example, that certain scientific discoveries had not been made in 1500 and thus that a viewer then would not have perceived the work with those in mind. People can imagine, with effort, what it must have been like to experience a work without such knowledge. There is a great difference, Savile argues, between misunderstanding and not fully understanding. He accuses many contemporary theorists of either confusing the two or failing to prove that misunderstanding is always operative. "The strongest claim that follows from the premises we are given is that we cannot ever *guarantee* that we have *not* been infected in the way suggested, but this is a long way from saying that such infection is inevitable."[35]

Savile says that people are able to make adjustments when they approach works created by someone else or in some period or culture other than our own. This notion seems right to me. We can see that the dog signifies loyalty, the bagpipes sexuality. That is, we can asssign a meaning from the past to our own reading. The message of the Gothic arch can certainly be seen as reaching to and for a God even by those who do not believe in Him. People who prefer simple, sleek lines to richly ornamented scrolls can still appreciate the scrolls if they make an effort to understand the decorations as an achievement of a period with attitudes and tastes we can imagine having.

In a sense, Savile's criticism is like Sebastian's in the quotation at the opening of this chapter. "Does anyone feel the same kind of emotion for a butterfly or flower that he feels for a cathedral or a picture?" Bell intends this as a rhetorical question. When Sebastian refuses to concede to Bell's authority, the position flounders. Similarly, those who believe that we can never interpret a work might be asking, "Can anyone today ever see Steen's pictures as his peers did?" Savile has essentially responded, "Yes, I can."

SUMMARY

Art objects figure in aesthetic theories both as existing independently or as requiring a context without which they could not exist. Analogously, aesthetic experience has been viewed as properly focusing on intrinsic formal properties of things (colors, shapes, rhythms) or as involving in significant ways features or conditions that lie beyond the object itself. History, social institutions, ideologies, and, in my own theory, traditions have all been identified as influential or essential to the nature of art and the aesthetic. Though formalists rightly claim that attention must be paid to formal properties, they are wrong to restrict too narrowly the considerations relevant to aesthetic experience. Both content and context matter as well.

In expressing their different points of view, several of the theorists we have encountered referred to the meaning of a work. "Getting" a work means understanding and appreciating it. In the next chapter we shall examine problems that surround interpretation and criticism.

NOTES

1. Benedetto Croce, *Aesthetics as Science of Expression and General Linguistic*, trans. Douglas Ainslie, 2d ed. (London: P. Owen, 1967); see also John Hospers, "The Croce-Collingwood Theory of Art," *Philosophy* 31 (1956): 291–308.

2. Richard Wollheim, *Art and Its Objects* (New York: Harper & Row, 1968).

3. Joseph Margolis, "Works of Art Are Physically Embodied and Culturally Emergent Entities," in *Culture and Art*, ed. Lars Aagaard-Mogensen (Atlantic Highlands, N.J.: Humanities Press, 1976), pp. 32–44.

4. David Pole, "Presentational Objects and Their Interpretation," *Philosophy and the Arts*, Royal Institute of Philosophy Lecture Series 6, 1971–72 (London: Macmillan, 1973) pp. 147–64.

5. Roger Fry, *Vision and Design* (London: Chatto & Windus, 1920), p. 23.

6. Ibid., pp. 36–37.

7. Clive Bell, *Art* (London: Chatto & Windus, 1914), p. 25.

8. Roger Fry, "The Artist and Psychoanalysis," in *The Hogarth Essays*, ed. Leonard S. Woolf and Virginia Woolf, 1924; reprinted (Freeport, N.Y.: Books for Libraries Reprint Series, 1970), p. 297.

9. Mario de Michelli, *Cezanne* (London: Thames and Hudson, Dolphin Books, 1968), p. 19.

10. D. W. Gotshalk, *Art and the Social Order* (Chicago: University of Chicago Press, 1947), p. 115.

11. W. K. Wimsatt, *The Verbal Icon* (London: Methuen, 1970; first published 1954), pp. 21–40.

12. *Dutch Painting of the Golden Age* (The Hague: Royal Picture Gallery, 1982), p. 112. Reprinted by permission.

13. John Berger, *Ways of Seeing* (London: Penguin Books, 1972), p. 84.

14. Ibid., p. 88.

15. Walter Benjamin, "The Work of Art in the Age of Its Technical Reproducibility," in *Illuminations*, ed. Hannah Arendt, trans. H. Zohn (New York: Schocken Books, 1969).

16. Terry Eagleton, *Marxism and Literary Criticism* (London: Methuen, 1976), p. 8.

17. Kendall Walton, "Categories of Art," *Philosophical Review* 79 (1970): 334–67.

18. Ibid., p. 343.

19. George Dickie, *Art and Aesthetics: An Institutional Analysis* (Ithaca, N. Y.: Cornell University Press, 1974), p. 34. Dickie has made revisions of the definition following the ensuing discussion of it. However, because it has been most widely scrutinized in this form, I shall stick with it. For more recent articulations, see *The Art Circle* (New York: Haven Publications, 1984).

20. Ibid., p. 37.

21. Ted Cohen, "The Possibility of Art: Remarks on a Proposal by Dickie," *Philosophical Review* 82 (1973): 69–82.

22. Ibid., p. 72.

23. Richard Wollheim, "The Institutional Theory of Art," in *Art and Its Objects*, 2d ed. (Cambridge: Cambridge University Press, 1980), p. 160.

24. Ibid., p. 165.

25. Arthur Danto, "The Artworld," *Journal of Philosophy* 61 (1964): 571–84.

26. Danto develops this theory in detail in *The Transfiguration of the Commonplace* (Cambridge, Mass.: Harvard University Press, 1981).

27. Ibid., p. 124.

28. P. F. Strawson, "Aesthetic Appraisal and Works of Art," in *Freedom and Resentment* (London: Methuen, 1974), p. 180.

29. Marcia M. Eaton, *Art and Nonart* (East Brunswick, N. J.: Associated University Presses, 1983), pp. 96–122.

30. Claude Lévi-Strauss, *The Savage Mind* (London: Weidenfeld and Nicholson, 1962), p. 29. For other structuralist discussions, see Yury Lotman, *The Structure of the Artistic Text* (Ann Arbor: University of Michigan Press, 1976); Jonathan Culler, *Structuralism and Poetics* (London: Routledge and

Kegan Paul, 1975); and David Robey, ed., *Structuralism: A Reader* (Oxford: Oxford University Press, 1970).

31. Jacques Derrida, *Of Grammatology*, trans. G. Spivak (Baltimore: Johns Hopkins University Press, 1976); and *Positions*, trans. Alan Bass (Chicago: University of Chicago Press, 1981).

32. Geoffrey Hartman, Introduction to *Deconstruction and Criticism* (New York: Seabury Press, 1979), p. viii.

33. Anthony Savile, *The Test of Time* (Oxford: Clarendon Press, 1982), p. 21.

34. Ibid., p. 44.

35. Ibid., p. 45.

CHAPTER 6

Interpretation and Criticism

What was my surprise, then, on taking [the novel] up with a group of students, to discover that not one of them interpreted it as I did. My faith in what seemed to me the obvious way of taking the story would have been shaken, had I not, on explaining it, found the majority of my fellow readers ready to prefer it to their own. And this experience was repeated with later groups. Yet, even after several years, it had not occurred to me that what seemed the natural interpretation of the narrative was not the generally accepted one among critics, however little it might be among students. And then one day I ran on a comment of Mr. Chesterton's on the story. He took it precisely as my students had. I began watching out in my reading for allusions to the story. I looked up several references to it. They all agreed. Evidently my view was heretical. Naturally I asked myself more sharply than ever why I should take the tale as a matter of course in a way that did not seem to occur to other readers. Was it perversity on my part, or profundity?

H. C. Goddard |

The quotation above comes from an article on Henry James's short novel *The Turn of the Screw*.[1] I have chosen it for several reasons. For one thing, in it we find allusions to many of the issues central to philosophical questions about the nature of interpretation and criticism—the topics of this chapter. I have also cited Goddard because the work that he is discussing provides a marvelous case study—for it has been the object of an incredible amount of interpretative and critical controversy. Furthermore, I believe Goddard is an excellent critic—and I would like to try to explain what excellent criticism is—where *criticism* is to be understood as the assessment that something is good as well as bad, that is, not always negative.

Initially we can understand *interpretation* to cover activity that has as its goal the description or explanation of what a work is—what it means, or what properties or characteristics it has. By *criticism* we shall first mean the evaluation or assessment of something—in particular judging whether something is good or bad. We shall look at whether there are correct and incorrect interpretations and criticisms and at whether there are facts to which we can appeal when we attempt to justify our descriptions and assessments of art and aesthetic objects.

THE NATURE OF INTERPRETATION

A Puzzling Case

In Chapter 5 we saw that a significant and influential group of theorists believes that we can never interpret completely or correctly what others say or write. If we cannot interpret a work—say what it is—it follows that it is meaningless to try to say whether it is good or bad. Other theorists believe that this is nonsense—that we can and do explain and evaluate (with varying degrees of difficulty) all the time.

Professor Goddard taught English at Swarthmore College for many years, long before we began to be worried by the deconstructionist suggestions that the classroom is disastrously like a slave/master situation. He was in the business of introducing students to reading, understanding, and appreciating literary works. He chose Henry James's *The Turn of the Screw*, as have hundreds of his English-teaching colleagues and, he tells us, was continually surprised that his first reading of that novel, one he thought obvious, was not the first reading of his students. It was not just that their interpretations differed over details or generated shades or nuances of meaning. They differed radically.

For those of you not familiar with the short novel in question, I shall provide a summary. This is not easy (and I do not want to spoil your reading), for one's interpretation colors how it is summarized. In its prologue, guests at a Christmas gathering are exchanging ghost stories. One of the guests says that he can top them all—but that he must first send for a manuscript that he says was given to him by his sister's governess. When it arrives, he reads it aloud. (It is taken down by the narrator, and thus we have a three-tiered tale: governess, guest, narrator. This itself has been the focus of much critical discussion.) The governess has been hired by the uncle of two children who live on a country estate. The man lives in London and wants to be freed of all responsibility for the children, so he asks the young woman to take it all upon herself. She is attracted to him and, with great intensity, undertakes to do what he requests. Shortly after arriving at the estate, the young woman comes to believe that it is haunted by two evil ghosts and sets out to protect the children from them. In the process the children become terrified; in the end the little girl flees with a housekeeper, and the little boy dies in the arms of the governess.

As Goddard has, I have used the novel in class, and each time there have been wildly divergent readings. Some students believe that the story is a straightforward ghost story. (This is the initial reading of Goddard's students.) Others believe that the ghosts are the creation of the governess's imagination. Both readings lend themselves to variations. The ghosts are (1) real and (a) are a real danger to the children or (b) are in cahoots with the children, and all four symbolize evil and corruption over which the governess triumphs. Or the ghosts are (2) not real but (a) the result of the governess's sexual frustration, (b) the results of general Victorian repression, or (c) the result of the housekeeper's suggestions.

Goddard's reading is a version of 2a. Although his students when told of his reading were persuaded by it, he found that other critics read it as the students first did—a simple ghost story. He began to wonder if his interpretation were profound or perverse (and, if the latter, one imagines he must have worried about what he was doing to his poor students).

Several questions are raised by this dilemma, and trying to answer them has occupied many philosophers of aesthetics. Is Goddard's reading correct? Or, if not correct, is it nonetheless a better reading? Is it possible for someone to have a good, but incorrect interpretation—one that provides the reader with a great deal of satisfaction but is inconsistent with the way most experts describe a work? Why do Goddard's students change their minds? What must or can be done to settle the question of whether what the governess says is true or false? Is there any objective basis for determining whether the novel is or is not a straightforward ghost story or for deciding whether it is a good or bad novel? James himself said that the story was just a ghost story. Some critics who prefer the other reading try to show that he was intentionally deceptive when he made such statements. But suppose we believe he was telling the truth. Must we then read the novel as a ghost story, even if we believe that it is better if read as a psychological thriller? If an expert's interpretation that is different from mine yields less pleasure for me, why should I ever accept it?

Good and Correct Interpretations

One way to justify an interpretation different from the artist's or the experts' (or even a friend's) is to say that it provides us with more pleasure. We might admit that the writer intended to produce a ghost story, but still insist that reading it as a psychological study of sexual repression is more aesthetically satisfying.

We can, for example, distinguish between *good* and *correct* interpretations and acknowledge that the two sometimes diverge. This will allow us to retain the freedom to look aesthetically at things in our own ways, while acknowledging that others may stick more closely to the artist's intentions or to the work as it is more generally understood. Someone might admit that James meant *The Turn of the Screw* as a ghost story and that the words do constitute a ghost story, but insist that he or she gets more of an aesthetic kick from the text when it is read according to Freudian analysis. We could thus understand someone who said, "I know my interpretation is not the standard one, but it is better for me; mine is good though probably incorrect."

Understanding or getting the meaning of something straight is usually a matter of knowing what the words or other symbols mean. Sometimes, especially when the vocabulary is unfamiliar, we have to go to dictionaries or other sources (like Ripe's *Iconologica* cited in Chapter 4), hoping that this will help us to determine what the correct interpretation is. Of course, we are free to ignore such facts as the seventeenth-century meaning of a word or a nineteenth-century musical practice, if we believe a better interpretation is obtained by sticking to twentieth-century meanings; "better" here means "yields more pleasure."

Or, if we want a correct interpretation, we may have to know what the artist intended. Then if we think we know what James was doing, we will take his reading seriously. We often want to learn what people we believe are in a position to know have to say about things. Consulting artists' own statements about their work is not just a sign of timidity or intimidation, though it can be this. Usually we consult them because we think that what they have to say will be helpful and will bring a fuller appreciation of a work.

The question of "correct interpretation" has been applied to several contemporary transcriptions of music written in earlier centuries. The classical performer Andrés Segovia and Leo Kottke have both played Bach's "Jesu, Joy of Man's Desiring" on the guitar, and Walter Carlos's "Switched-On Bach" provides a synthesizer version. Some people believe that Segovia's is most true to Bach's orchestral version and thus better than Kottke's twelve-string rendition or Carlos's electronic production. Fans of Kottke and Carlos often say that "truer" and "better" are not the same. Some who insist on a correct interpretation argue that the original work simply disappears when we can no longer hear human voices reacting and interacting with an orchestra. Others claim that the work is still there and provides much, if different, pleasure when reproduced however one chooses.

If we do not want to limit ourselves to a *correct* account of a work's content, we are free to disregard any information that might determine which of several conflicting interpretations is correct. (Here, "correct" means consistent with the author's intention or an established standard.) If, for example, we want to get as much aesthetic pleasure from a work as possible, and believe we can get it by forgetting what scientific discoveries had been made or what musical instruments were available in a certain period, we can provide our own idiosyncratic interpretations.[2] But are we doing something "wrong" if we do so?

The Lack of Facts

If what we are after is a correct interpretation, we must try to "get the facts" about a work's production to determine what it really means. The problem with many works of art is, of course, that we are often not in a position to determine once and for all whether a claim is true or false. Given his Scandinavian ancestry, we may want to claim that Hamlet had blue eyes. Given the genetic dominance of brown eyes, it may be more reasonable to believe that they were brown. Which view is correct? There is no place in Shakespeare's play *Hamlet* where his eye color is mentioned. There seems then to be no *fact* of the matter.

Philosophers use the word *underdetermined* to describe statements for which there is insufficient evidence. A claim is underdetermined if we cannot say whether it is true or false because there is nothing that will settle the matter. Given the underdetermined nature of *Hamlet* with respect to eye color, it may not be plausible to believe either that Hamlet's eyes were blue or brown. Nothing in the play settles this question. Of course, *if* we come across another portfolio with a revision of *Hamlet* in which Shakespeare has him say, "Oh, that these too, too bright blue eyes would close," that would seem to settle the matter. The newly discovered play would be a more complete version of the same play. Of course, one can object that it does not make any difference what color Hamlet's eyes are. But many underdetermined items are not so inconsequential; they are directly relevant to interpretive puzzles. Nowhere in *The Turn of the Screw* does the governess or any other character explicitly state that she was crazy. If we were to come across a version of the novel in which the governess's reports are no longer underdetermined (she says, for example, "Of course, I was crazy at the time"), it would no longer be the same novel. Even to speak of a "different version" here seems incorrect.

The philosopher Robert J. Matthews believes that we must distinguish between *description* and *interpretation*.[3] Because we often cannot *settle* (or finally determine) the matter with respect to an interpretation, we are less certain about our claims. Our descriptions, however, can be definitely determined because they depend upon things in the work to which we can directly point. We *describe* the governess as a young woman, and *interpret* her as sexually repressed. Description depends upon being able to know if what we say about a work is true or false. Interpretation depends upon being in a position to know whether what we say is plausible, reasonable, or defensible.

The problem, of course, is trying to decide which of several interpretations is plausible. Rarely can we point to one feature of a work to settle the question of which interpretation is the most reasonable. *The Turn of the Screw* is fascinating because the questions it raises cannot be settled easily. Critics make their various cases by pointing to a variety of things: the artist's life, the text, dictionaries, artistic practices in the period, and psychological theories with which James might have been familiar. Critics even disagree about which of these things are reliable sources. (As we saw in Chapter 2, some think that intentions are out of bounds in interpretations, for instance.)

Some theorists have decided that it is useless to try to come up with either correct or plausible interpretations. They conclude that interpretations are purely a matter of subjective opinion. Others, however, reject this and maintain that even in the face of lack of what we might call "hard facts" some interpretations can be shown to be more nearly correct than others. It will become apparent later that I favor this latter view.

The Possibility of Objectivity

John M. Ellis, a literary theorist, believes that saying that interpretation is "underdetermined" is based on a confusion.[4] Of a claim made by David Frost about the president's Watergate activities, Richard Nixon said, "That's just an interpretation." He meant that Frost was saying something about which he could not be certain and could never prove. Ellis thinks critics do not "just interpret" in this sense.

Ellis believes that some critics have tried to avoid making interpretative and evaluative claims because they have mistakenly viewed what other critics do as unleashed speculation ("just an interpretation"). The former have instead tried to turn criticism into a more genuinely empirical activity by restricting themselves to facts that can be objectively described. For example, in the hope of becoming truly scientific, they count words to determine authorship. (As with fingerprints, the frequency with which individuals use particular words can be used for identification.) According to Ellis, the belief that one can become "scientific" by distinguishing facts from interpretations and sticking solely to facts is to misunderstand completely both the nature of criticism and the nature of science.

One lesson of modern science, and of the philosophy of science, is that observations and theories cannot be neatly separated. Statements of facts embody theories and vice versa. Scientists constantly move back and forth between theory and fact. Both outside and inside of academic science—that is, in our daily lives as well as in more sophisticated investigations—we are not neutral observers. Our theories color our observations.

The philosopher of science Karl Popper writes, "I do not think it is helpful to express the difference between universal theories and singular statements by saying that the latter are 'concrete' whereas theories are *merely* symbolic formulae or symbolic schemata; for exactly the same may be said of even the most 'concrete' statements."[5] Our minds are not blank tablets upon which information is written while we stand passively by. Our minds, to use a Popperian metaphor, are more like searchlights; theories and concepts already formed influence what we actively look for and then discover in the world. There is no hard, fast line that separates facts (what is out there in the world) from theories (what is in here in our minds).

What is true of science is also true of art. We saw in Chapter 4 that E. H. Gombrich (who credits Popper's influence on him) and Nelson Goodman describe looking at art as a kind of reading; habits and theories that we bring with us determine what we see or hear. Describing and interpreting are not separable if what we see or hear involves decoding. Richard Wollheim discusses an interesting example of another sort of interconnectedness. In *Macbeth* some of the title character's speeches are incoherent. Some critics have attributed this to grammatical ignorance, others to deep psychological disorder. The text itself does not settle the dispute; no simple description of what is going on can be given, for how one describes the text will depend upon one's interpretation.[6] One could *repeat* the text—that might be neutral—but then one would not be *describing* it.

When the deep connection between description and interpretation is not understood, Ellis says, "Both parts of the cycle are devalued, and the critic is set free to say whatever he wants to say."[7] I think Ellis is quite right about this. The sort of distortion that has led creationists to puff themselves up by claiming that evolution is "just a theory, too," has too often characterized critical relativism and the view that any old interpretation is as good or bad, just as objective or subjective, as any other.

"An interpretation is a hypothesis about the most general organization and coherence of all the elements that form a literary text," says Ellis.[8] The best interpretation is the most inclusive. Observation and interpretation are carried on (and out) simultaneously. Hypotheses direct attention, which then may come up with things that make us revise our hypotheses. Ellis's view is certainly born out in practice. Students report experiences such as the following with regard to *The Turn of the Screw*: "Suddenly I noticed that no one else saw the ghosts." Readers form new hypotheses as they go along and consequently notice new things—the governess's nervousness, for instance.

Justifying an interpretation is not merely a matter of being able to point to a body of facts to support a claim. The facts must be organized and often supplemented by reasonable hunches. It is impossible to come up with clear (let alone hard and fast) rules about what constitutes the best interpretive strategies. But, says the philosopher David Pole, there aren't *rules* for the best ways of doing science or philosophy either. As Savile does (see Chapter 5), Pole believes that artworks are public objects with a history and that they invite interpretation. They can be *mis*interpreted, especially if their history is ignored. Often critics act as frustrated artists, "producing variations on a theme—a thing harmless in itself."9 They read or put more into a work than they read or get out of it. This practice becomes harmful when they confuse what they are doing with giving a correct interpretation.

Two things encountered in art call for an interpretation, according to Pole. First, sentences or features sometimes make no sense, and we want them to. We have no idea what the words mean, or why there is a bagpipe in a painting of a Dutch interior. Consulting a dictionary or an iconologica like Cesare Ripe's may help here. Second (and more typically), objects make sense, but we want to know how special effects are achieved. We are not just interested in whether the governess actually sees ghosts, or if the man with the pipe is doing something evil. We want to know what James does to produce suspense or how Steen conveys the feeling of lively camaraderie. We want to explain why these works are as good as they are. This calls for something quite different from going to reference books.

Many people have claimed that we need to give *reasons* for why a particular work of art affects us, how it is effective. Thus the role and nature of reasons in art criticism has received a great deal of attention. We shall return to this topic later (see "Reasons in Criticism"). First, we shall examine the differences between interpretation and evaluation.

Separating Interpretation and Criticism

Ellis believes that some contemporary theorists mistakenly believe that they can be scientific by avoiding interpretations and sticking to descriptions. The philosopher Stein Haugon Olsen believes that a similar mistake is made if we think we can separate interpretation and evaluation and stick only to interpretation. The view that value judgments are unempirical, he says, has led many contemporary theorists (Northrop Frye, for example) to try to do without them—to be, instead, empirical and descriptive only. But this separation cannot happen because, as Olsen notes, "Value considerations determine the very nature of interpretive judgments."10

People who believe that interpretation and evaluation can be separated usually do so because they think the first is required for the second—interpretation must be carried out (if not completed) before evaluation can begin. We must, to echo

Plato (Chapter 2) know what is being done before we can know if it is being done well; we must know what x *is* before we can say whether it is a *good* x. Recall that such an attitude lies behind Kendall Walton's contextual theory (see Chapter 5).

The possibility of separating interpretation and evaluation is an important issue. In an article examining reasons given in support of interpretations, Charles L. Stevenson gives the following examples of various reference sources: dictionaries, other works by the same artist, revisions of the work, or simply an acknowledgment that a work is better if interpreted in one way rather than another. The last example, he says, "reminds us that the interpretation and evaluation of a poem are rarely separable steps in criticism. We do not first *interpret* it and then evaluate it, taking each step with finality. Rather we test a tentative interpretation by considering the tentative evaluation of the poem to which it leads, progressively altering works in the light of the other."[11] (Again we see parallels with scientific activity.)

Sometimes when we ask what a work means we want to know what the artist meant. But this is not always or even most often the case. According to Stevenson, a better construal of the question is, "What does it mean to someone or to a particular group?" It is difficult to specify the group; it doesn't mean "the average person" or "the experts." The group can only be described, he believes, in *evaluative* terms: *best, proper, ideal, skillful,* and *sensitive.* What does a poem mean, for instance, to an ideal reader? The kind of criticism that we engage in presumes beliefs we have about what features make a group (or us) "ideal" or "sensitive."

This is why interpretation itself is evaluation—not because it concerns evaluations of particular works but because it concerns how we think we should look at works. We can distinguish giving reasons for an interpretation and giving reasons for giving that sort of reason!

Stevenson believes that we can show that something is a good or a bad standard to use in interpreting artworks, though he admits that evaluations are open-ended. We can give reasons for the relevance of an artist's intentions or our reliance on dictionaries or iconologica. Put simply, it is reasonable in general to refer to intentions when we explain human action and products of that action. It is reasonable to consult dictionaries when we want to explain what something means. Such methods of explanation are usually reliable and people should try to apply them whenever they can. Some methods, on the other hand, are "indicative of habits of mind that no one *ought* to have, as Stevenson says.[12] Distorted perspective or obsessive attention to just one sort of feature is not a characteristic of a well-rounded, reasonable person, let alone a good critic. Concentrating on sexual repression alone, for instance, is not a good way to live—or to look at art.

Stevenson assumes that critical activity (and the criticism of critical activity) consists of giving reasons. Others have argued that this is not what critics do. I shall try to show that even when giving reasons does play a role, criticism does more; it invites people to pay attention to special things.

THE NATURE OF CRITICISM

How Can Criticism Help?

In the preceding chapter, we considered some theories based on the belief that the complexity of contexts radically underdetermines meaning—that is, that we can never know what someone else means. In the first section of this chapter, we saw how a lack of hard facts and rules makes it difficult to decide which of several different interpretations of an artwork is correct. We can never be sure that someone else reads or sees or hears a work in the same way as we do. We can never know that others will enjoy what we enjoy. This uncertainty has led some people to conclude that criticism—if it is construed as giving reasons for saying that something is good or bad—is a waste of time. Such people don't stop talking about art; they just deny that a goal of their discourse is proving that their preferences should be shared.

Other people believe that criticism not only doesn't help (in transmitting knowledge or sharable experiences) but that it is positively harmful as well. They fear that critics (particularly academic critics) intimidate, browbeat, and brainwash. Such critics warp or stifle completely our own responses to things, displacing them with their own arrogant, self-interested biases. In our society, readers (if they don't give up reading altogether) feel compelled to read introductions for fear they will misread the novel. They demand elaborate program notes at concerts. And when people go to museums, they either plug themselves in to casette recorders or spend more time *reading* the identification cards on the walls than *looking* at the pictures hanging there.

Though there is some truth to this assessment, many of us continue to believe that criticism can help. Sometimes, at least, it seems to lead to a better experience. Respecting the insights of others, we believe that they bring us to see things we would have missed if left on our own. Without having read Kenneth Clark's article on Rembrandt's self-portraits, I don't think I would have noticed how much the painter emphasizes the nose. Had I not learned a vocabulary for categorizing gables on old Amsterdam buildings and a chronology for their development, I am certain that I would have overlooked much about the city's architecture—and consequently would have missed having certain aesthetic experiences.

The question that I want to raise then is not *does* criticism help, but *how* can it help? Instead of giving a precise definition of 'criticism', I shall indicate some features that are central to critical activity.

Reasons in Criticism

Whether or not interpretations and evaluations are finally, theoretically separable, critical writing does include both. Consider these two statements: "In Michelangelo's *Moses*, Moses has just overcome the impulse to throw the tablets to the ground" and "A highlight of your visit to Rome will undoubtedly be Michelangelo's statue of Moses." In both cases we expect the speakers to explain and support what they say. Generally when asked "Why do you say that?", we give answers construed as *reasons*. But do critics actually give reasons? Is that how they help? Do they give us reasons for taking what they say to be true and hence for believing what they say and for reacting in the same ways that they do?

Paul Ziff correctly points out that while some of the things people say about artworks and aesthetic objects are offered as reasons for a work's goodness or badness (for example, "It's disorganized"), not all are (for example, "It was recorded in Minneapolis").[13] Although he believes that evaluation and interpretation can be separated, Ziff thinks that critical reasons, when they are really reasons, are directly relevant to both. "To say a painting is a good painting is here simply to say it is worth contemplating," he notes.[14] Critical reasons *point* to things that can be perceived and at the same time *direct* our perception. Aesthetic response or involvement is an activity. We don't just see or hear; we look and listen. Thus something apparently quite trivial such as, "It is completely flat," if it "tells us what to do with the work," can become a reason.[15] That is, if a remark about a work gives us an instruction or suggestion that helps us notice interesting things about the work, then the remark gives us a reason for noticing and appreciating that feature. It gives us a reason for valuing the work.

Ziff cautions that we must, however, be careful about what "us" includes. At most we can only predict what we or our friends will find worthy of contemplation. There are no general laws about what people think or find worthy of aesthetic attention. Thus what counts as a *reason* will be relative to certain groups of individuals.

The art historian Jakob Rosenberg disagrees. He believes that quality is a matter of common agreement among all sensitive, trained people. He is confident that a careful study of the history of criticism will reveal general reasons that can be given in support of aesthetic judgments.[16] He has studied the history of criticism in an attempt to discover the best critical strategies and norms.

Rosenberg admires the sixteenth-century critic Vasari for introducing systematic criticism—criticism that in Vasari's case involved assessment based on truth to nature, *invenzione* (understanding of life), and *designo* (form, drawing). However, he is critical of Vasari's rejection of whole periods of art (the medieval, for example), for he thinks this blinds us to individual works that are valuable. Rosenberg chooses Roger de Piles as an exemplary representative of seventeenth-century French criticism, and one is struck by the *quantitative* nature of his system. De Piles's analysis derived from grading artists on four components—composition, drawing, color, and expression—on a scale of one to twenty. Rafael won with the following score:

composition	drawing	color	expression
17	18	12	18

Other scores are as follows:

Michelangelo:

8	17	4	8

Titian:

12	15	18	6

Caravaggio:

6	6	16	0

(So much for one of my favorites!) What Rosenberg admires in de Piles's study is the inclusion of so many masters, thus making use of direct comparisons as well as providing an objective basis for evaluation.

Rosenberg goes on to survey eighteenth-, nineteenth-, and twentieth-century criticism. The point of his study is to highlight merits and defects of landmarks of criticism, thus enabling us, by identifying what is best about them, to formulate objective standards for critical methodology. He believes that inclusive comparative historial studies of art show that general criteria of excellence exist, namely artistic economy, selectiveness, feeling for the media, sense for the significant, consistency, vitality, inventiveness, intensity, clarity, and expressiveness. All have been, and continue in the twentieth century to be, things for which critics must look and which they can use to justify their evaluations.

The formulation of objective critical standards that Rosenberg holds as the goal of criticism is precisely what comes under attack in "Critical Communication," a very important essay by Arnold Isenberg. Isenberg argues that most people (and he would include Rosenberg) misunderstand the real nature of criticism.[17] It is not, he thinks, a reason-giving activity. His argument is quite appealing and bears careful attention, though I shall restate it in my own way and use my own examples.

Typically we understand giving reasons according to the following model:

C (Claim): "It must be raining."
You ask "Why?"

R (Reason): "Because the streets are wet."

Now if R is a reason for C, then the two statements have to be connected. Generally they are tied together by a law, or at least by a lawlike generalization:

L (Law): When the streets are wet, it's (usually) raining.

Is this, Isenberg asks, how criticism works? His answer is no. Consider the critic Constantine Leontiev's remarks about *War and Peace*:

> I love, I even adore *War and Peace*, for being a gigantic work and for its bold introduction into the novel of whole sections of philosophy and strategy, contrary to rules of artistic restraint and accuracy that have governed us for so long. I love *War and Peace* for the patriotic fervor that at times burns in its pages so fiercely, for the moving depictions of battle, for powerful charm in the representations both of the "temptations" of the world and of the joys of family life, for the variety of characters who conquer the reader's mind, and for their endurance.[18]

We might simplify this passage according to the above model in the following way. (Isenberg uses *verdict* for *claim* and *norm* for *law*.)

V (Verdict): "*War and Peace* is wonderful."

R (Reason): "*War and Peace* has moving battle scenes."

N (Norm): "Anything with moving battle scenes is wonderful."

But N just doesn't work—even if we insert the qualifier "usually." As hard as critics and theorists have tried, Isenberg believes, they haven't discovered any lawlike generalizations tying together verdicts and reasons that even most critics agree on. It is not true that most novels with moving battle scenes are wonderful, let alone that most wonderful novels have moving battle scenes. And it doesn't help to try to make the norms more complicated or inclusive—it has moving battle scenes, charming representations of family life, *and* patriotic fervor. Even if we admit with Rosenberg that historically such things as vitality, intensity, or clarity have repeatedly been used to support critical judgments, Isenberg believes that no norms can be formulated that will enable us to connect our verdicts with reasons.

Critics, Isenberg says, thus *cannot* be in the business of producing deductive arguments. They do not give *reasons* in support of their claims. In fact, they don't get us to *believe* anything at all. Rather they are in the business of *pointing*. They get us to *perceive* some features of an object or event.

William G. Lycan and Peter K. Machamer offer one criticism of Isenberg's theory.[19] They argue that if the critic's role is to get us to perceive what he or she has seen, it is difficult to know how we would ever tell if he or she has been successful. Good criticism cannot just be getting the viewer to have *some* perception; the critic is after a particular perception. Because perceptions are private, individual experiences, how can we know when the viewer's experience matches or approaches the critic's? Just looking in the right direction or uttering the same words will not prove it. Isenberg is trying to explain critical *communication*, but Lycan and Machamer worry that we have no grounds of calling it 'communication' at all according to his view.

According to Lycan and Machamer, critical reasons have a special logic. They do connect generalizations (norms) and evaluations (verdicts), but not because the generalizations have been scientifically discovered. Reasons are part of our language; we have learned to call works of art "good" when we can also say that they are "balanced," "graceful," "unified," or "suspenseful."[20] Unless we share the language of the speaker, we will probably not be able to know what she is talking about or pointing to when she talks about unity or plot development. When we do speak the same language, we understand that these features are important. (This is perhaps one reason that critical discourse often seems so confusing. Critics talk about "form," "balance," and "unity," and people often claim that they do not understand what the critics are talking about. Understanding why unity is a good thing and understanding what unity is go together, according to Lycan and Machamer.)

Even if Lycan and Machamer are right that a term such as "unified" means, in part, that it is a good thing for a work to be, "The second movement of Beethoven's Third Symphony is unified" does not by itself imply "The second movement of Beethoven's Third Symphony is good." The most we can say is, "To the extent that Beethoven's Third Symphony is unified, it is good." But critics seem to want to make more general claims—to say straightforwardly that the second movement is good.

One way to show that Isenberg is wrong is to come up with some norms. But I share Isenberg's doubt about the possibility of devising norms. Experience indicates that we either produce something false or something empty: "Novels with battle scenes are good" or "Works with all and only good qualities are good." I do believe, however, that we can show that Isenberg is only partly right in his overall characterization of critical activity. But first let us look at another reason for thinking that criticism is a kind of pointing.

Transferring Critical Judgments

Alan Tormey has given another version of the theory that critics do not have belief, but perception, as their goal.[21] He uses Jaako Hintikka's distinction between "self-sustaining propositions" and "indefensible propositions." A *self-sustaining proposition* or statement has this form: If a knows that b knows that p, then a knows that p. If Jones knows that Smith knows that Shakespeare wrote

Hamlet, then it follows that Jones knows that Shakespeare wrote *Hamlet*. An *indefensible proposition* or statement has this form: If Jones knows that Smith believes Ringo Starr is a guitarist, it does not follow that Jones knows Ringo Starr is a guitarist.

The proposition "If a knows that b judges that p" is clearly not self-sustaining, according to Tormey. Nothing follows about Jones's judgments from her knowledge about Smith's judgments. If I know that you judge that *Hamlet* is a good play or Ringo Starr a great drummer, my own judgment is not affected.

Tormey believes that the reason for this lack of transfer is that a critical judgment assumes *acquaintance* with the object. I must perceive for myself in order to judge if a symphony is unified or a painting balanced. I won't even trust your reports of your judgments, let alone take them as my own, unless I am certain that yours is an eyewitness account. If you tell me that the newly discovered organ works of J. S. Bach are the best he ever wrote and I later learn that you have neither seen the score nor heard them performed, I will not take your remarks as your judgment. I will expect that you have just been reporting the judgment of someone else, the *New York Times* critic, for instance.

So aesthetic judgments, according to Tormey, cannot be transferred.[22] Does it follow that they cannot be verified? Tormey believes that critical judgments are claims that are "open to test." The tests themselves are eyewitness accounts. What we have are "*corroborative* tests, and the *case* for a critical judgment rests on the extent of its acceptance among independent judgers not on something like 'degree of confirmation'."[23]

Nor are critical judgments disconfirmable the way that scientific judgments are. No single counterexample falsifies them. Counterclaims simply fail to corroborate critical judgments. If you judge *Hamlet* to be a good play, and I don't like it at all, neither of us proves that the other is wrong. One of us simply fails to contribute to general acceptance about the play's value. Nor can critical claims be the basis of prediction—as, Tormey thinks, the past shows us. What is approved or disapproved in one era will not always be true. I cannot even be sure that my best friend, who usually corroborates my judgments, will tomorrow enjoy the movie that I delight in tonight.

However, it does not follow that judgments cannot be defended, according to Tormey. Judgments also are not merely summaries of what people in certain groups enjoy—like statements about the goodness of "Porsches and pineapples"—things that are the objects of fads or fashions or mere personal preference. Special *methods* must be used and evidence of their use must be available before critical judgments can be taken seriously. Tormey says, "The good critic is therefore someone who is able to *formulate* such judgments for our scrutiny."[24] The writer who described *The Way You Hear It* for us in Chapter 5, tried to do so in such a way that our judgment would corroborate his own. He *pointed* to the youth pouring wine in the hope that we would, like him, judge this as a means of unifying the painting's composition. This is why "x is good" by itself is poor criticism. It doesn't help us in our effort to contemplate a work nearly as much as statements about moving battle scenes or unifying minor seconds or a painting's balanced color scheme. Thus, as Isenberg does, Tormey believes that enhanced perception is the goal of criticism.

Criticism as a Report of Feelings

One of the reasons that critical judgments apparently are not transferable or predictable is that we seem never to be sure that others will feel as we do about a movie or a song or a painting. This doubt has led some theorists to maintain that, when all is said and done, evaluation is really just a matter of expressing personal feelings. Leontiev may mention suspenseful battle scenes or tender depictions of family life, they argue, but he is finally just telling us that he adores *War and Peace*.

Is criticism primarily a matter of expressing personal preferences? Are critics mainly in the business of telling us how they feel?

Remember that according to Isenberg, if I am asked to give reasons for my belief that *War and Peace* is wonderful, I have to reply, "I can't. I don't have any reasons." I find that quite unsatisfying. Even if Ziff is right that my reasons may not be your reasons, it does seem that *I* have some. Critical activity in Isenberg's view seems to become completely arational—not based on reason at all (and asking for reasons is irrational—contrary to reason). Many will share my feeling, I think, that it is dissatisfying to conclude that we engage in arational behavior when we make critical judgments. (Admittedly not everyone will feel this way; some may take great delight in it.) It is helpful, I believe, to compare the sorts of things we say about artistic and aesthetic objects with the sorts of things we say when we are ready to admit that we are simply, arationally, reporting our feelings.

I lived in Denmark for a while and was quite surprised to discover that almost everyone I met disliked peanut butter. Whenever anyone said, "Peanut butter is awful," I was inclined to ask, "Oh, why do you think so?" At the same time, I was not really surprised when they were unable to give reasons. If they responded, "I don't know, I just don't like it," I did not think that they were irrational. And their arationality did not seem inappropriate.

Is our reaction to *War and Peace* like this? Perhaps it is to some extent. Perhaps there are arational aspects of our aesthetic preferences. We reach a point when all we seem able to say is, "I just like this sort of thing, but I don't expect everyone to be like me." We don't, however, reach this point immediately as we do when we talk about peanut butter or raw oysters or turnips. Otherwise we should be amazed that so much has been written about *War and Peace* and so little about peanut butter. Surely all this talk must have a purpose. We don't care that Leontiev adores the novel. If criticism were just a report of feelings, we would not bother to read it.

Criticism as Pointing and Inviting

Isenberg says that criticism is pointing. He might say that there is more discussion of *War and Peace* than of peanut butter because there is more to point to. Nonetheless, we should not dismiss one as irrational for failing to like *War and Peace* anymore than we do for failing to like peanut butter.

Certainly pointing things out is a very important part of criticism. Kenneth Clark's essay on Rembrandt can be looked at as an elaborate way of pointing to (among other things) Rembrandt's nose in his self-portraits. But I think it is more than that; and Ziff's distinction between recognition and contemplation suggests what more it is. If criticism were just pointing, then it would appear that the corresponding response on the part of the critic's audience would be something like recognition. A critic points to the nose or the repeated use of a minor second, we see or hear it, and that would seem to be that. But there is more to criticism than this pointing—at least when criticism is truly effective. We go on to see more for ourselves; we continue on our own.

John Ellis says that the best criticism is the most inclusive, but he does not have a simple quantitative standard in mind. The things pointed to must relate to the coherence and organization of a work. To use Ziff's terminology, good critics do not bring us just to recognize the nose, but to contemplate it. We scrutinize it, Tormey would say. We consider how it works as an organizing force, Ellis would say. All three have the same notion in mind. Critics point to *significant* details, to those details that, once seen, allow us and provoke us to continue on our own to view the work.

Thus in addition to pointing, critics *invite* us to look for things. Different critical approaches invite us to do this in different ways or to look for different types of things. *The Turn of the Screw* has been criticized from supernatural, psychoanalytical, religious, metaphysical, and historical standpoints. A kind of game is played with the text, and we are invited to join in the game. It is a bit like getting the knack of a series of numbers (2, 5, 9, 14, 20 . . .); we learn how to continue to fill in the blanks ourselves. We are stimulated into looking for things on our own.

Children's magazines often have a page where their readers are asked to "find the missing pictures." They love it. (So do most adults.) Critics ask us to "find the Freudian allusions" or "find the religious symbols," or "find the absences." It's fun—usually. But just as looking for the cup in the tree stops being fun after a while if we think there isn't one there at all, so the critical game becomes frustrating when we decide that only by distorting the text can we find repressed sexuality or the Prince of Darkness.

Criticism is an invitation to engage in activity that we have reason to believe is pleasant. If criticism were a matter of trying to *reason* people into taking *pleasure* in something, then it would be doomed. But this is not the only possible role of reason in criticism. The *rational* aspect of criticism occurs when we have reason to believe that what is being pointed to, what we are invited to do (to look at and for) brings pleasure. Suppose I say, "Here's a good seascape," and you reply, "No, it isn't." "But," I go on, "it has balanced composition." "I see," you answer, "but I still don't like it." Here I am wrong not about the balanced composition (though it is, of course, possible to be wrong about this) but about your liking it or finding it pleasing. Nonetheless, in a culture in which many (perhaps even most) people enjoy balanced compositions, it is rational to expect that others will appreciate having that quality pointed out.

Tormey says that we must have direct acquaintance with an object before we can know if it is good. I think this way of putting it blurs an important distinction. Of course, one cannot actually be pleased by something if that something isn't there to please. In aesthetic experience, pleasure comes from actually experiencing objects or events. To the extent that critical judgment involves actually being pleased, direct acquaintance (the presence of the object or event) is required.

However, as I recently read guidebooks in preparation for a trip to northern Belgium, I said things like, "There are beautiful sixteenth-century buildings in Bruges." I was not trying to fool my husband into thinking I'd been there before—he knew I hadn't and I knew he knew I hadn't. But I think I was as certain that there are beautiful sixteenth-century buildings in Bruges as I was that there are sixteenth-century buildings there. How can this be so?

Although critical judgments cannot be the basis of predictions about what people a hundred or a thousand years later will like, they can be used, I think, to make shorter term predictions. Suppose my brother flies by helicopter over the Upper Susitna river in Alaska and writes, "You're going to love this river. It abounds with white water." Isn't that a full-fledged, *rational* prediction? What is the basis of my certainty about beautiful buildings in Bruges or of his certainty that I will delight in the Upper Susitna river? Past experience and knowledge about others' reactions provides ground for prediction here just as it does in science.

We cannot be *reasoned* into taking pleasure, but we can have *reasons* for believing that things will be pleasurable. Besides being reports of pleasure actually taken (hence the necessity of direct acquaintance), critical judgments also involve assumptions about what other people find delightful (or its opposite). My predictions will sometimes be very narrow and only involve myself or close friends. I give Henry James novels only to a small group of people. I have one friend whom I know will not read anything longer than two hundred pages. On the other hand, some predictions are quite inclusive. With confidence I call almost anyone's attention to a cardinal seated on a wintery branch or to the clever use of the clock in *High Noon*.

Something like empirical generalization is involved in our beliefs about what people like. If most people, most Russians, most readers of the *New York Times*, are known to delight in moving family scenes, critics will point them out. They know what to invite their particular audiences to look for.

We cannot have complete confidence that actual feelings of pleasure will take place. I may be sick or in a rotten mood and not enjoy the Flemish buildings or white water that I travel miles to see. Yet confidence does extend to the belief that this is the sort of thing that people of a certain (limited or extensive) type will delight in. That certain things are aesthetically pleasing may be part of our concept of what it means to be rational. (What Stevenson says about "habits of mind" earlier in this chapter is relevant here.) But, of course, proof of this would be very difficult and complex.

Susan Bernick compares critical activity to social work or therapy and contrasts it with other sorts of treatment, for example, medical treatment of pneumonia.[25] In order for criticism, like therapy, to do any good, the critic/therapist has to know more about the patient's life than a doctor treating pneumonia does. Criticism/therapy can only help when we are able to see the things pointed out to us and to act upon them. In the case of criticism, action amounts to continuing on our own to notice features and organize and relate them. Like therapy, criticism can help only if we want it to—only if we think that other people's insights and eyes and ears can help us to participate in activities that we will find rewarding.

Goddard's criticism of *The Turn of the Screw* stands out because he is a superb pointer and a superb teacher. He regards us as "fellow readers" and shows us how to go on to contemplate and scrutinize in ways that will produce delight. He does not have to distort the text in order to get us to see things hidden in it. He does not try to force his views; indeed, in the paragraph I quoted at the beginning of this chapter he expresses humility and readiness for exchange of insights. He is a good "inviter."

Good criticism results in a fuller, richer aesthetic experience by ferreting out the aesthetic value of objects and events. Now, in the final chapter, we will consider what aesthetic value is.

SUMMARY

A major problem with aesthetic interpretations and criticisms is the extent to which they are justifiable. When people interpret and criticize objects and events, they are often asked to explain or support their judgments. Sometimes people admit that their views are idiosyncratic—directed primarily at increasing personal pleasure. At other times they attempt to point to objective facts to show that their opinions are correct. Although the existence of "facts" in this area and the very possibility of objectivity have been hotly debated, I have suggested that shared ideas and values within a culture provide a basis for rationally justifying interpretations and evaluations.

Philosophers of aesthetics have also worried about the nature of interpretive and evaluative activity. Some have thought that the two must be kept clearly distinct; others have insisted that this is impossible. The role (or lack of it) of giving reasons in critical activity is another subject of controversy. Some philosophers argue that successful criticism leads to the sharing of beliefs and judgments between critics and viewers; others have argued that criticism is a complex way of pointing or inviting viewers to attend to special features of objects and events. I have argued that both giving reasons and pointing are strategies for inviting others to attend to things that people mutually value.

| NOTES

1. H. C. Goddard, "A Pre-Freudian Reading of *The Turn of the Screw*," *Nineteenth-Century Fiction* 12 (1957): 3-4.

2. For more on this topic, see Marcia M. Eaton, "Good and Correct Interpretations of Literature," *Journal of Aesthetics and Art Criticism* 29 (1970-71): 227-33.

3. Robert J. Matthews, "Describing and Interpreting a Work of Art," *Journal of Aesthetics and Art Criticism* 36 (Fall 1977): 5.

4. John M. Ellis, "Critical Interpretation, Stylistic Analysis, and the Logic of Inquiry," *Journal of Aesthetics and Art Criticism* 36, no. 3 (Spring 1978): 253-62.

5. Karl Popper, *The Logic of Scientific Discovery* (New York: Basic Books, 1969), p. 59.

6. Richard Wollheim, *Art and Its Object*, 2d ed. (Cambridge: Cambridge University Press, 1980), p. 88.

7. Ellis, "Critical Interpretation," p. 256.

8. Ibid., p. 258.

9. David Pole, "Presentational Objects and Their Interpretation," *Philosophy and the Arts*, Royal Institute of Philosophy Lecture Series 6, 1971-72 (London: Macmillan, 1973), pp. 150-51.

10. Stein Haugon Olsen, "Value Judgments in Criticism," *Journal of Aesthetics and Art Criticism* 42, no. 2 (1983): 135.

11. Charles L. Stevenson, "On the Reasons That Can Be Given for the Interpretation of a Poem," in *Philosophy Looks at the Arts*, ed. Joseph Margolis (New York: Scribner's, 1962), p. 124.

12. Ibid., p. 135.

13. Paul Ziff, "Reasons in Art Criticism," in *Philosophy and Education*, ed. I. Scheffler (Boston: Allyn and Bacon, 1958), pp. 219-30.

14. Ibid., p. 221.

15. Ibid., p. 226.

16. Jakob Rosenberg, *On Quality in Art, Criteria of Excellence, Past and Present* (Princeton, N.J.: Princeton University Press, 1967).

17. Arnold Isenberg, "Critical Communication," *Philosophical Review* 58 (1949): 330-44.

18. Constantine Leontiev, "The Greatness and Universality of *War and Peace*, in the Norton Critical Edition of *War and Peace* (New York: Norton, 1966), p. 1389.

19. William C. Lycan and Peter K. Machamer, "A Theory of Critical Reason," in *Language and Aesthetics*, ed. B. R. Tilghman (Lawrence: University Press of Kansas, 1973), pp. 87-112.

20. For a fuller analysis of this logic, see Lycan and Machamer, "A Theory of Critical Reason," pp. 97-99.

21. Alan Tormey, "Critical Judgments," *Theoria* 39 (1973): 35-49.

22. Tormey thinks, incidentally, that this is an important difference between aesthetic and ethical judgments. If you tell me about what someone has done, I can judge for myself that he is evil without having to see it. But no matter how much you tell me about an artwork, I cannot make judgments until I have the chance to look or hear for myself.

23. Ibid., p. 43.

24. Ibid., p. 47.

25. Susan Bernick, unpublished manuscript.

Aesthetic Value

*Not only is enormous labour spent on [art],
but in it, as in war, the very lives of men are
sacrificed. Hundreds of thousands of people
devote their lives from childhood to learning
to twirl their legs rapidly (dancers), or to
touch notes and strings very rapidly (musicians), or to sketch with paint and represent
what they see (artists), or to turn every phrase
inside out and find a rhyme to every word.
And these people, often very kind and clever
and capable of all sorts of useful labour, grow
savage over their specialized and stupefying
occupations, and become one-sided and self-
complacent specialists, dull to all the serious
phenomena of life and skillful only at rapidly
twisting their legs, their tongues, or their
fingers.*

Leo Tolstoy, *What is Art?* ❙

Why do or should people spend time and money on artistic and aesthetic
pursuits? Why are works of art and aesthetic objects important to us? Why do we
want to have aesthetic experiences? How do aesthetic experiences stack up against

others—are they a luxury, or are they essential to a meaningful life? Answering these questions requires a theory of aesthetic value, and conversely an adequate theory of aesthetic value should provide an answer to the questions. In this chapter we shall look at two kinds of theories of aesthetic value. The various versions of each typically point to benefits that individuals derive from aesthetic activity, but as we shall see, there are serious contemporary problems that require us to give attention to potential social benefits as well.

Leo Tolstoy was concerned that art and artists in his society (late nineteenth-century Europe) were becoming more and more corrupt. In the quote that opens this chapter, he expresses his contempt for time and energy wasted in the pursuit of meaningless activity. Figure 5 shows an object that I think Tolstoy would have despised, for it exemplifies what he thought was wrong with what he described as the "pseudo-art" or "counterfeit art" of his day. It lacks what he considered genuine aesthetic value.

Before looking at why Tolstoy would have reacted negatively to the vase, think about your own reaction. Suppose it were dropped and shattered. Would you think that any real or permanent harm had been done? Would there be less *value* in the world? What kind or kinds of value might be destroyed or decreased?

Typically, this vase would be classified as "decorative art," because it has purely, or primarily, decorative value. It does have a function of sorts—holding tulips—but even that function itself is decorative and could be fulfilled by something less elaborate.

The vase has sizable *economic value*, though exactly what dollar figure should be attached to it is a matter of speculation. We could only determine its current market value is by putting it on an auction block, but it is unlikely that the vase will be sold, for it is part of the collection of the Loo Palace (part of the Dutch Rijksmuseum) in Apeldoorn, Netherlands. That palace was formerly used by Queens Wilhelmina and Juliana, beloved Dutch rulers. Hence the vase has some *sentimental value*, and it might have *historical value*. It has some *art historical value*, because it demonstrates a special technique and design. As a cultural artifact, it might also be used to tell us something about the cultures in which it was made and subsequently preserved and hence said to have *cultural value*. The vase seems to lack *religious* or *ethical value*, for looking at it probably will not produce better people. And even if we grant the economic, historical, or cultural values, it still seems correct to say, "It's not really good for anything—except to look at." Does *aesthetic value* boil down to the pleasures of perception?

A distinction is often made between "inherent value" and "consequential value." Things that have *inherent value* are prized for themselves alone; things with *consequential value* are prized because they produce or lead to something else that is valued. Is aesthetic value to be understood as the value something has in itself independent of any other purposes or interests? Or is aesthetic value derived from or dependent upon some other kind of value—moral, economic, scientific, or historic? Or is aesthetic value a mixture of both? After discussing examples of

Figure 5 Flower vase with bust and monogram of King William III (1650–1702), Rijks-museum Paleis Het Loo, Apeldoorn, The Netherlands. Used by permission.

inherent and consequential approaches, I shall propose a theory of aesthetic value that, I believe, combines the best features of each approach. We shall then see whether these theories help us to decide whether individuals and societies should spend time and money in support of aesthetic activity.

INHERENT AESTHETIC VALUE

One way of explaining the importance of artistic and aesthetic objects and events is by pointing to features in them—shapes or colors or rhythms—that are intrinsically valuable. However, most theorists believe that *experiences* of these things are valuable, not the things in themselves. That is, in a world in which no one was around to experience colors or shapes, it is doubtful that they would be valuable.

Therefore aestheticians who favor theories of inherent value generally locate the value in the experiencer and argue that the experience is valuable in itself, not because it leads to something else that is valuable. We do not ask ourselves what the vase can be used for, whether we can learn anything from it, whether selling it could finance a college education or feed a hundred people for a year, whether looking at it will make anyone a better person. We just look at *it*, think about it alone, in isolation from everything else. We concentrate on its shape or on the way the lines of the design interweave and relate to one another and to the spaces. If we enjoy these things, the vase has aesthetic value; if we do not, it does not. The reason that we contemplate works of art or aesthetic objects (such as sunsets) is simply that we derive pleasure from their inherent properties.

Experiences that are pleasurable (and perhaps memories of them) have immediate value—inherent value that can be separated from our normal concerns. When we looked in Chapter 3 at some views of aesthetic experience that characterized it as distanced or removed from everyday practical concerns, we saw that Jerome Stolnitz identified the aesthetic as contemplation of something for its own sake. Thus his is clearly an inherent view of aesthetic value. Many have agreed with him. Stuart Hampshire says:

> The spectator-critic in any of the arts needs gifts precisely the opposite of the moralists; he needs to suspend his natural sense of purpose and significance. To hold attention still upon any particular thing is unnatural; normally we take objects—whether perceived by sight, touch, hearing, or by any combination of the senses—as signs of possible action and as instances of some usable kind; we look through them to their possible uses, and classify them by their uses rather than by sensuous similarities.[1]

Hampshire's view that aesthetic experience is unusual implies that it is valued apart from any uses to which it can be put. By distinguishing aesthetic experience from ordinary or practical experience, inherent theorists ensure that the value of aesthetic experience will not be connected with or depend upon practical experience. Aesthetic value is freed of any dependence upon the (good or bad) consequences it has in other areas of human experience.

Monroe Beardsley, another proponent of an inherent theory of aesthetic value, characterizes the aesthetic as gratification arising from experience of formal unity and regional qualities (colors, shapes, and patterns) of objects and events.[2] Both are qualities *in things*, but the value lies in the gratification that people take in these qualities. The objects are the instruments through which pleasure is obtained, and aesthetic value is solely dependent on the pleasure that accompanies perception, not on the experience being of any further use to the perceiver.

According to Beardsley, an aesthetically valuable vase or sunset or ballad provides an experience in which attention is intensely, coherently, and completely directed at regional qualities. Thus he defines 'aesthetic value' in the following way:

> 'x has aesthetic value' means 'x has the capacity to produce an aesthetic experience of a fairly great magnitude (such an experience having value)'[3]

Rankings are possible, for just as one can explain that this car is better than that one because it gets better gas mileage or steers better, so one can say that one vase is better than another because it provides a more intense or more coherent experience than other vases.

What characterizes inherent theories of aesthetic value then is the insistence that what matters, what makes something aesthetically good, is the way it makes people feel. We do not have to worry about anything else—about money or virtue or truth. We are free simply to "Enjoy!"

CONSEQUENTIAL THEORIES

In our own century, inherent value theories have had the ascendancy, but if we look at the entire history of Western thought, consequential theories are more frequent. Plato, for example, was very critical of art and artists because he thought neither contributed to our knowledge of reality. Believing that an experience can be worthwhile only if it contributes beyond itself to a more rational life, he was suspicious of artists who seemed to him to ignore the proper business of life. (Artists tend to work through inspiration rather than according to intelligible rules and principles, he believed). Lacking valuable consequences, art is worthless; as an obstacle to rationality, art is positively harmful.

Aristotle had a much higher opinion of art because he believed it does contribute to a better life by satisfying human needs and desires. In particular, art is important because, when successful, it brings us knowledge. Good tragedy, for example, teaches us about human behavior and experience; it shows us how certain kinds of people tend to act in certain sets of circumstances. He also believed that art provides us with an emotional outlet and thus has therapeutic value. Aristotle sees value where Plato sees none, but they agree that value depends upon fulfilling a particular function such as teaching or bringing about emotional release. Hence both philosophers have consequentialist theories of aesthetic value.

As Plato did, Tolstoy believed that something was deeply amiss in the art of his culture.[4] But, unlike Plato, he thought it *possible* for art to be and do good. I am sure that Tolstoy would have scorned the tulip vase. It is precisely the sort of thing that shows how bad things have gotten, he would have complained. It is valued only because it gives us pleasure, and that is to misunderstand completely the real value that art can possess.

Tolstoy used an analogy to food to explain a confusion he thought accounted for the prevalence of counterfeit art and a misunderstanding about what constitutes real value. Just as people might mistakenly take the value of food to be the *pleasure* it gives, so some people confuse the value of art with the pleasure it gives. Clearly the real value of food is *nutrition*; individual items are good or bad just to the extent that they contribute, or fail to contribute, to a healthy body. Even those who "live to eat" finally must admit this. Art, like food, is *really important*, and it could not be, Tolstoy reflected, if all it did were to give us pleasure. Its real value must lie in the contribution it makes to a healthy individual and a healthy society.

Tolstoy found the food analogy useful because he thought it suggests *where* a confusion is likely to rise, not just *what* the confusion (nutrition/pleasure) is. According to Tolstoy, the materialistic upper classes, removed as they are from the actual meaning of life, view food as a source of pleasure. The lower classes, whom Tolstoy idealized, realize what the value of food actually is. Similarly, it is the corrupt elite (those likely to purchase vases like the one in Figure 5) who think pleasure is all-important. Their counterfeit art fails to accomplish the real goal of art: expression of emotion that unites people in feelings of community with one another. The art of commoners communicates sincere feeling, according to Tolstoy, and hence has genuine value.

Tolstoy failed to realize—or to admit—that even people who are forced to eat only nutritious food usually prefer something "tasty," at least occasionally. What is true of food may well be true of art. Thus the analogy is not very helpful. However, locating aesthetic value in moral consequences or in what we can learn is at the core of contemporary consequentialist theories of aesthetic value. Attempts to account for people's positive attitudes toward aesthetic activity in terms of goodness and of truth have much in their favor.

Ethical and Aesthetic Value

Ethical theories can be roughly divided into those that define 'good' in terms of adherence to a principle (such as doing one's duty) or in terms of consequences (producing happiness, for example). The former are called "deontological," the latter "consequentialist." Theorists of consequential aesthetic value try to show that aesthetic value is derived from moral value—that artistic or aesthetic experiences lead people to understand and follow moral principles or to act in ways that bring about desirable consequences.

Contemporary theories in which aesthetic value is explained as deriving from moral value are much more subtle than Tolstoy's version. They do not claim that all art has a moral function or that there is an inevitable connection between being a person who enjoys sunsets and symphonies and being a virtuous person, or vice versa. Rather, the claim is that some art (masterpieces, usually) affects the way we look at the world. Such art doesn't just sharpen our seeing or hearing, but expands our awareness of the human situation and thus produces people who are likely to follow acceptable moral rules or strive to produce favorable results.

In Chapter 5 we looked at Anthony Savile's view of criticism and interpretation as historical—requiring that people imagine what the context that produced a work must have been like. He believes that this imagining spills over into everyday activities. People who read great novels or listen to beautiful symphonies are better able to put themselves in others' shoes because they understand them and their world better. Art provides this understanding, Savile asserts:

> We cannot give a coherent account of planning for the future unless we have available notions like "desirable," "valuable," or "estimable." . . . This can come about only if we find things in the world to be of value and to be worthy of our esteem, and that will happen only if we frame a vision of the world that sees it from a point of view that we share with others and that generates descriptions of it cast in terms of, and responsive to, our common interests.[5]

The philosopher of science Hilary Putnam makes a similar claim about the effect of art. It does not give us scientific truth, he thinks, but a kind of moral truth:

> If I read Céline's *Journey to the End of the Night*, I do not *learn* that love does not exist, that all human beings are hateful and hating (even if—and I am sure this is not the case—those propositions should be true). What I learn is to see the world as it looks to someone who is sure that hypothesis is correct. . . . But all this is not empirical knowledge at all; for being aware of a new interpretation of the facts, however repellent, of a construction that can—I now see—be put upon the facts, however perversely—is a kind of knowledge. It is knowledge of a possibility. It is *conceptual* knowledge.[6]

Clearly theories such as those of Savile and Putnam can be empirically confirmed or disconfirmed. If people who spend much of their time reading and listening to music do not turn out to be more virtuous than those who never or rarely engage in aesthetic activity, then the value attributed to such activity is discredited. Even if *great* artworks teach people to see the world in ways that make them more sensitive to moral principles and the consequences of their actions (as Putnam claims Céline's work does), we are still left to account for the value some might want to attribute to lesser works—the tulip vase, for instance. It is difficult to see how our looking at and enjoying the vase will help us to become more responsive to the needs or attitudes of others.

If works of art and aesthetic objects do not produce good (or bad) people, then aesthetic value must either be inherent or derived from some other source. The same conclusion follows according to some theorists who concentrate not on the morality of the audience but the morality of the artist. Claiming that artists' actions are not open to moral evaluation, they argue that what artists do and produce must be assessed in something other than moral terms.

We saw earlier that Stuart Hampshire distinguishes ethics and aesthetics on the grounds that in aesthetic situations the observer's normal concerns are put aside—something that clearly does not happen in ethical situations. He also believes that artistic problems are special. Artists set their own problems, he thinks, and this makes aesthetic situations quite different from moral situations in which problems are set for us. What Hampshire has in mind is this notion: All of us share moral concerns—whether to permit abortion, how to share wealth, or when it is essential that we tell the truth, for example. The problems artists face—whether to write in a major or minor key, how much blue to use, whether to tell a tale from the point of view of an outsider or insider, for instance, are different:

> [An artist] has his own conception of what his own work is to be. Even if his work must satisfy some external demand, he has his own peculiar conception of it. . . . He has therefore created his own technical problems; they have not been presented to him; they arise out of his own conception of what he is to do.[7]

The difference is like one between our decision whether or not to help someone who is drowning or whether to dress punk or preppy.

If artists do exclusively set their own problems, then it would appear that the *value* of what they do lies outside of the realm of moral assessment. If what they do is viewed in terms of choices between major and minor keys, red or blue, and first- or third-person narrative, then it is hard to see how they can be held morally accountable. Maybe the person(s) who made the tulip vase *should* have done something else (tend the sick, for example), but surely the decision to use blue instead of red paint is not open to *moral* criticism.

However, we load the story when we limit description of artistic activity to choices about technical manipulation of a medium. Artists also make choices about the feelings or ideas they want to express or communicate. Increasingly, they are evaluated on this basis.

Consider this poem by John Donne, "Go and Catch a Falling Star":

> Go and catch a falling star,
>> Get with child a mandrake root,
> Tell me where all past years are,
>> Or who cleft the devil's foot,
> Teach me to hear mermaids singing,
>> Or to keep off envy's stinging,
>>> And find
>>> What wind
> Serves to advance a honest mind.
>
> If thou be'st born to strange sights,
>> Things invisible to see,
> Ride ten thousand days and nights,
>> Till age snow white hairs on thee;
> Thou, when thou return'st, will tell me
> All strange wonders that befell thee,
>>> And swear
>>> Nowhere
> Lives a woman true, and fair.
>
> If thou find'st one, let me know;
>> Such a pilgrimage were sweet,
> Yet do not; I would not go,
>> Though at next door we might meet.
> Though she were true when you met her,
> And last till you write your letter,
>>> Yet she
>>> Will be
> False, ere I come, to two or three.

The poem contains a view of the nature of women: They are fickle creatures incapable of fidelity. Some readers insist that the view of women presented here is false—and harmful, because it perpetuates dangerous attitudes that lead to unfair treatment of women. For them, the poem is not amusing or clever, it is disgusting; and the *aesthetic* value of it is to that extent diminished. The artist should have portrayed women differently in this poem.

Of course, the poet might be excused on the grounds that he was simply expressing the common view of women—that he cannot be blamed for the attitudes that prevailed in his culture. Or one might say, it's just one poem, probably not read by all that many people—and when it is, it is read by people who can separate the ideas and the poetic technique, and their aesthetic experiences center around the latter. Or perhaps the writer was simply being playful—not seriously advocating the view that the dramatic speaker presents.

There are, nonetheless, art objects that are not so removed from the public eye or not simply playful. Pornography has recently become the focus of legal attention as an area where civil rights and freedom of expression apparently conflict. It is also an area in which we can see how moral and aesthetic evaluation become harder and harder to distinguish clearly from one another. Some people maintain that exposure to pornography tends to entrench men's false ideas of women and thus perpetuates abusive treatment. Something that makes people immoral, they insist, cannot have any kind of positive value. If John Donne could be excused because he was a creature of his times, or just being playful, contemporary photographers do not deserve the same consideration when they distort depictions of women to fit their own warped fantasies. They are not (or should not be) free to set their own problems. Contrary to what Hampshire says, their activity is as open to moral assessment as anyone else's. Even if artworks all by themselves do not turn bad people into good ones, or vice versa, artworks contribute to the development and perpetuation of moral attitudes. If some artworks reinforce undesirable attitudes, it is difficult to excuse their creators by saying that their problems are removed from the moral arena. According to supporters of this position, aesthetic and moral value cannot be separated ultimately.

Formalists, as we saw in Chapter 5, insist that genuine aesthetic experience is directed to intrinsic properties of things—and thus they consider moral effect (or lack of it) irrelevant. Theirs is clearly an inherent value theory. Contextualists are more inclined to connect moral and aesthetic value, for they tend to explain objects and experiences of them in broader ways. I shall argue later that people cannot separate moral and aesthetic concerns. But moral value is just one source from which consequentialist theorists derive aesthetic value. Another source is suggested by Putnam when he says that we become more sensitive through discoveries of truths that art presents.

Truth and Aesthetic Value

Plato's suspicion that a life given over solely to the pursuit of pleasure is not really valuable is shared by many people in our contemporary culture. Plato thought that we should always seek truth, and Aristotle provided a basis for its value by acknowledging a role for truth in art. In our century several writers have explained art's value in this way.

In Chapter 4 we looked at the question of whether or not art objects contain truth. Here we ask, Suppose they do (or can); so what? To what extent is the value of, say, a poem connected to the assessment of the truth of claims it contains? If we do not care whether poems contain true or false statements, it would seem that aesthetic value does not depend upon truth.

Consider again "Go and Catch a Falling Star" by John Donne. As we saw, it contains a specific view of the nature of women. To what extent will our agreement or disagreement with this position influence our assessment of the poem? If you believe women are fickle, will that cause you to like it? If you don't, will your belief make you dislike the poem? Would you like the poem more if it made a less extreme claim—if it asserted, for instance, that only some women are fickle?

Douglas Morgan argues that aesthetic value should not be undermined or diminished by treating it as a species of scientific or cognitive value.[8] Artworks do often contain or imply truths, he thinks, but this is not the basis of our aesthetic judgment of them and hence is not the locus of aesthetic value. Sometimes individuals agree with the view of the world presented, but find an artwork inferior, perhaps boring, badly composed, or trite. Sometimes they disagree with the view expressed, but delight in the work, finding it balanced, vivid, or witty. Furthermore, he says, questions of truth often simply do not arise; people at a concert do not turn to a neighbor as they applaud and say, "How true!" We often sing words we would be embarrassed to utter. I doubt anyone has asked whether our tulip vase is "true."

Morris Weitz agrees that sometimes truth is irrelevant to aesthetic assessment, but he believes that claims made in artworks are aesthetically relevant to some works.[9] (Notice that the question is not whether containing claims of truth makes something valuable in general, but whether such claims contribute to their *aesthetic* value.) If we put aside the problems of imaginary people, places, and events, important questions about truth remain. Works contain what Weitz calls "commentary"—generalizations about the world. He says that Proust's novel *Remembrance of Things Past* contains these generalizations: "Disenchanted men content themselves with the pleasures of loving rather than with any expectations from the beloved" and "In love we cannot but choose badly." (Perhaps that's the problem with the speaker in the Donne poem!) Recall that some people think that in viewing art the viewers simply put aside ordinary questions of truth, but Weitz thinks this is wrong. They do consider truth or falsity, and because this is part of the aesthetic experience, it must be related to art's value. Assessing the truth is a part of the activity of reading literature (and perhaps of viewing art generally) and a source of the pleasure we derive from it.

Morgan suspects that this attitude grows out of an overemphasis on truth that results in "warping our talents, blinding our senses, and too narrowly channeling our hearts."[10] Nonetheless, he does have another type of consequential account of the value of art—one that I think combines considerations of truth and goodness. Without demanding assessment of art in terms of truth or practical consequences, Morgan nonetheless relates aesthetic value to the idea that art seems to develop our senses (seeing and hearing primarily). Thus aesthetic experience is not valuable just because it is pleasurable; it is valuable because people who partake of it become more sensitive, more imaginative, he observes.

A similar view was developed by I. A. Richards: "The value of the experiences which we seek from the arts does not lie . . . in the exquisiteness of the moment of consciousness; a set of isolated ecstasies is not sufficient explanation."[11] He finds it inconceivable that the value of art (poetry was his particular interest) can be reduced just to the pleasure it gives—even if we allow for pleasures relived through our memories. He denies, as Morgan does, that art has straightforward cognitive or scientific value, but he attributes psychological advantages to it: Poetry "organizes our impulses."[12] Great poetry, he thinks, helps us to develop and expand our attitudes, and therefore it makes us more sensitive human beings. Thus we are led back to a *moral* interpretation of aesthetic value.

In this section we have looked at various ways of explaining the value of aesthetic objects. Some theories locate this value in the experience we have as we contemplate them; if the experience is good (pleasant), the thing or event is valuable. But these theories seem to ignore contributions that art makes in other areas of human experience. Consequentialist theorists relate aesthetic value to things that lie somewhere beyond our immediate experience. They try to show that the consequences of our contemplation are good, that we learn something or become better or more sensitive people. I shall later suggest a way of relating inherent and consequential value.

At the beginning of this chapter, I suggested that an adequate theory of aesthetic value will explain why people do or should engage in artistic and aesthetic activity. Although we may not agree with the answers given, inherent and consequentialist theories do propose that individuals benefit either directly or indirectly from the time and money spent in pursuit of aesthetic experiences. But we can also consider the *social* value of aesthetic objects and events. Our culture believes that aesthetically valuable things benefit society as a whole. Thus we establish museums, protect scenically beautiful resources, and support orchestras. These activities require public decisions. If they are *worth* supporting, it must be the case that society should spend time, energy, and money creating opportunities for aesthetic experience. Thus an adequate theory of aesthetic value should explain why society should devote its resources to aesthetic matters; and people who insist that society should provide citizens with aesthetically rich environments should be able to support their demands with a theory of value. Let's first consider some "applied" aesthetic problems that confront contemporary society (at least in affluent nations), and then I shall present my own theory of aesthetic value. I hope that it will meet the test of both answering questions about what communities should do aesthetically and support the answer with an adequate theory.

APPLIED AESTHETICS

Art and Public Policy

One area in which moral and aesthetic concerns come together was referred to in the discussion of aesthetic value interpreted ethically—the devaluing of art that abusively portrays women. Many people argue today that artists should not be given free reign—that they should not be allowed to exhibit publicly works in which the humiliation or torture of women is legitimized. Although much of the current debate about pornography concerns the issue of freedom of expression, many supporters of artists' rights point to the aesthetic value of what is produced. Censorship is obviously a public issue that extends beyond consideration of inherently pleasurable experiences to matters of resolving conflicts between freedom of expression and possible harmful consequences.

In the first chapter, I described a "work of art" that created a public uproar—the displaying of several boulders in downtown Hartford. Such controversies rarely are based on clearcut theoretical distinctions. Most of the people who objected to *Stone Field* probably did not stop to ask themselves whether their response was moral, aesthetic, or a mixture of the two. The same mixture—the use of 'ugly' and 'wrong'—marked my family's discussion of *Mother* (see Chapter 1). It is difficult to draw a line between moral and aesthetic value; for example, it's hard to ignore the feelings of the artist's mother even if we admire the painting. It is also difficult to separate the social consequences of displaying some artworks from purely aesthetic considerations.

Other serious aesthetic problems arise from cases that do not have such clear moral aspects or consequences—but do raise questions of public policy. The woman who lives across the street from me has two pink, plaster of paris flamingos in her front yard. They are incredibly ugly. I sometimes worry that the little children who pass by each day on their way to the school bus are having their aesthetic sensitivity spoiled! The statues certainly offend me and diminish greatly the pleasure I get when I look out my front window. Nonetheless, it is her yard, and in a free country she's free to display whatever she likes. There are some laws about public nuisances (like smelly garbage or unpleasant noises late at night), but courts are usually unwilling to extend these laws to aesthetically offensive exhibits on *private* property.[13] (However, the courts do seem increasingly willing to interfere here.)

But when works of art are displayed on *public* property and paid for with public funds, public agencies must involve themselves in decisions, and sometimes restrictions on freedom of expression are called for. Unfortunately, it is not always clear how such policies are developed or should be developed. Who should decide whether a statue or fountain should be erected in a public square? Should public funds be used to support the artists who produce such objects?

Most American cities lack clear procedures for dealing with proposals for beautifying main streets or neighborhoods. A theory of aesthetic value should suggest ways for handling public decisions about funding and displaying works of art and should outline strategies for "beautifying" public spaces.

In an outspoken article in *Journal of the Public Interest*, Douglas Stalker and Clark Glymour describe most public sculpture as "malignant objects."[14] They claim that most public art (art that is publicly financed and displayed) does little good and lots of harm and that the government (and hence all of us) should end its involvement with public art. Whatever *aesthetic* benefits accrue from such art are minimal; they affect only a small part of the public. "On the whole, the public does not like today's public art," say Stalker and Glymour, who cite letters to the editor as evidence.[15] Even artists themselves soon tire of a given style and move on to something else, leaving us with a bronze dinosaur-shape where we could have had a pool, shade tree, or a seesaw.

Stalker and Glymour go on to argue that the esoteric works usually created by contemporary artists do not engage the general public aesthetically or intellectually. Moreover, they positively humiliate viewers:

> Viewing public sculpture and finding it ugly or silly or simply commonplace, the common person brings his own eyes and mind into direct conflict with the judgment of the aesthetic and political authorities. He can only draw one of three conclusions: Either his own judgment is hopelessly flawed, so that he is a complete aesthetic incompetent; or else that of the authorities is flawed in a like fashion; or, finally, he and his fellow citizens have been made the butt of a joke by the artist, his associates, and his admirers.[16]

The only escape, the authors complain, is to "cultivate indifference" to the objects around us—surely not a reasonable goal of enlightened public policy.

Some people have responded that Stalker and Glymour overstate the case—that opposition is not as widespread as they believe.[17] Others argue that shaking people up is precisely the goal of contemporary artists. Some people favor plebiscites to decide what pieces should go where; others are horrified by this prospect—imagining, perhaps, cities dotted with hundreds of images of big-eyed owls or pink flamingos.

Another suggestion is that artists should feel a deeper sense of responsibility about their role in helping the public approach their work, especially when that public finances their activity. David Pole, for example, thinks that serious artists must not expect critics to do their work for them, but that artists must themselves help the public understand their work.[18]

Stalker and Glymour's argument turns on their belief that most public sculpture does not have aesthetic value in the eyes of the public it is supposed to serve. For them, *social* value depends upon aesthetic value: If the work provides aesthetic value (is beautiful, for example), then it has social value. However social values often come into conflict—moral or religious or economic values, for instance. The problem of balancing different values, particularly economic values, is clearly central to public policy issues. What is required is not just a way of determining whether something has aesthetic value but of comparing this value with other types of values. Serious attempts to develop strategies for doing this have been made in the assessment of environmental resources.

Environmental Aesthetics

The *beauty* of our environment has become a central concern in our culture only recently. Sometimes this concern is given an economic explanation: As our basic needs such as food and shelter are fulfilled, people have the leisure or freedom to look around. We have advanced from a society in which the environment was to be controlled and exploited to a society in which it can be enjoyed. Hence the environment should be made or kept enjoyable. This shifting attitude is exemplified in our laws, the most important of which is probably the National Environmental Policy Act of 1969. This law provides for the protection of certain areas and requires that environmental impact studies be carried out before projects that will affect our surroundings can be undertaken. It also has as a goal the protection and provision of "aesthetically pleasing surroundings." It describes aesthetic values as "presently unquantified" and requires the development and "utilization of a systematic interdisciplinary approach, which will ensure the integrated use of . . . environmental design arts in planning and decision-making."

This requirement has forced planners and decision makers to make aesthetic evaluations, but for the most part they have not turned to philosophic aesthetics for help. Nor do aestheticians and policy makers usually talk to each other. This is not surprising, because many contemporary philosophers of aesthetics have specifically asserted that they are not in the business of evaluation. In *Languages of Art*, for example, Nelson Goodman says that as he interprets and engages in philosophic aesthetics, he touches only incidentally on questions of value and does not provide canons of evaluation.[19] Since aesthetic impact studies clearly call for evaluation and action, environmental planners may reasonably be skeptical about getting much help from philosophers.

The requirement that due account be taken of the "presently unquantified" aesthetic amenities has led to frantic effort to quantify them.[20] These efforts range from fairly simple attempts to obtain a numerical score (for instance, asking hikers to assess a trail on a score of one to ten) to extremely complicated applications of sophisticated statistical methods and models (such as use of linear regression techniques to determine which factors—trees, water, hills—contribute to individual's preferences).

Although such studies give the appearance of objectivity because of the presence of numbers, they do not always give the information that they are legally supposed to give even when they are mathematically sound. Learning that 53 percent of hikers who use a trail in a given week give it a score of seven or above does not necessarily prove that the trail is *aesthetically* pleasing. The hikers may be evaluating it in terms of the physical challenge it presents or the upkeep of the path. A liner regression analysis may indicate that a group of people is pleased by trees over thirty feet high and eight inches in diameter, distributed in a ratio of six trees per fifteen square feet. It does not follow that the *cause* of their *aesthetic* delight is trees of that height, diameter, and density. They may view the stand as a good business risk or actually be aesthetically pleased by the proportions or play of light and shadow.

Many of the studies undertaken to carry out an aesthetic impact study are intuitively appealing. One of my favorites is a photographic method, in which people are given cameras and asked, for example, to take ten pictures of ugly things and ten pictures of beautiful things in a certain area.[21] Here, the use of 'beautiful' and 'ugly' does ensure aesthetically relevant results. (Actually many studies try to avoid such "loaded" terms, hoping thereby to be more objective. Surely this is a mistake; how can we know that we are assessing *aesthetic* response without using an aesthetic vocabulary?) Suppose we discover that everyone takes a picture of a particular weeping willow hanging over the shore's edge along a given stretch of river and includes it in their "beautiful" pile. Then perhaps we do know that this spot has aesthetic value and that we should take steps to protect that site.

Of course, such agreement is very rare, and when disagreement occurs, we must ask whether *everyone's* opinion is equal. That is, should only the people who use a trail regularly be surveyed? Only people trained in design? Local residents? Some campers are distressed if they encounter more than one other party in a day; others like to see other people. Should both groups have equal say about the development of wilderness recreation areas?

One (clearly consequential) way of discovering how much aesthetics matters when compared with other priorities is via economic studies.[22] We are accustomed to economic evaluation of the environment—a given area has a market value of, say, half a million dollars. We might try to give aesthetic experience this kind of quantitative basis. How much are you willing to *pay* to hike in a given area or canoe on a given river? How much office space will you sacrifice if you can have a "room with a view"? However, most of the problems with respect to the studies just described are encountered again here. Vacationing in a wild river region or having an office on the west side of a building may be a status symbol, so one's willingness to spend money or space for it may have nothing to do with aesthetic value. A parent on welfare may have no money to spend visiting scenic areas, but clearly that does not prove lack of aesthetic concern or sensitivity.

Psychologists have used another approach. Psychological environmental assessors do provide some theoretical basis for their projects. By fitting models for aesthetic evaluation into a larger picture of human behavior and response, they try to explain why and how certain features in our surroundings (trees or water, for instance) are connected to our aesthetic preferences. Such studies are typically perceptual or motivational. Perceptual studies are usually physiological and attempt to relate brain activity and emotions, for example. Motivational studies ground our aesthetic pleasure in the contributions an environment makes to basic human needs and interests such as survival or the urge for novelty. We like rivers, ponds, and fountains because we need water to survive, to give one simple example.[23]

Although most psychological studies are in the earliest, most primitive stages, they do, I believe, have the advantage of fitting aesthetic experience into human experience generally. I argued in Chapter 5 for a contextual theory of art, and I claim here too that we must consider the *context* of our aesthetic preferences if we are to understand them adequately. What can be called *humanistic* psychological and historical studies of aesthetic value as it is expressed in environmental or scenic preferences are preferable to the more narrow perceptual or motivational studies. Our appreciation of our surroundings, like our appreciation of works of art, has a history. Mountain or desert landscapes have not always been popular; it was only as people felt that they had controlled these environments to some extent that they came to be aesthetically appreciated. Aesthetic amenities cannot be given due consideration without explicit awareness of and attention to that history.

In a study of a pine barrens in New Jersey, two investigators discovered the following:

> Almost every person interviewed expressed concern and had concrete perceptions about the use of the landscape, whether for cordwood, sawboards, hunting and fishing, berry picking, wildflowers, or picnicking. The complexity of residents' visions of their landscapes in fact presented a problem because they neither could nor would separate what they saw from how they lived in and worked with their environment.[24]

Complexity of interests will always figure in human preference, though of course I would not describe it as a "problem." Our values and interests are integrated and interconnected. Aesthetic valuation does not take place in a vacuum, though we can *focus* on it and identify those elements that we usually concentrate on when we experience and enjoy a pine barren aesthetically.

People who are responsible for developing public art and environmental policies must have a fairly clear idea about what the aesthetic is and why it is socially necessary or desirable to provide opportunities for aesthetic experiences. One attempt to ground practical proposals in theoretic aesthetics is found in a study of the role of water in the landscape, where the inventory of relevant features (boundary definition, prominence, edge features) is justified by reference to Monroe Beardsley's analysis of the aesthetic in terms of unity and regional vividness.[25] (See Chapter 3.) Another group of investigators suggests that unity, composition, contrast, variety, balance, form, mass, shape, light, color, and rhythm be used because art critics and theorists refer to these properties.[26] The assumption in both of these studies is that regional qualities provide pleasure and that society benefits when its members are enjoying themselves. Consequentialists, of course, would insist that this is not enough, that considerations of goodness and truth also matter. Even if people like pine barrens or public sculptures, does this justify spending time, energy, and public funds for them? Or do we expect public funds and efforts to lead to benefits beyond pleasure?

A PROPOSED DEFINITION

If we are to be certain that due attention is being given to aesthetic value in formulation of public policy, then we must know first what the aesthetic is and then try to explain aesthetic value in terms of it. Quantifying aesthetic value, if that can be done at all, will only come later. To end this book, I will suggest what I think the aesthetic is and propose a view of aesthetic value that will help us justify both individuals' and societies' involvement in aesthetic affairs.

One recurring strain in the history of Western aesthetics has been an emphasis on the subjectivity of aesthetic experience. Aesthetic value arises from a positive response of a person or group of persons toward something. Whether we believe the response is natural or learned, whether we believe that only some responses are correct, or that some are better than others, it is obvious that unless someone *feels* positively inclined toward a thing or event, it cannot be said to have aesthetic value. (Consider the strangeness of "It's quite beautiful—but, of course, no one has ever liked it.")

Obviously this is not enough to distinguish aesthetic value from many other types of value. We must identify the special quality to which we respond favorably. Why do people who do preference studies go to trails or rivers where people canoe? This is not an accident; they do it because they assume that in our culture these things are valued aesthetically. Neither is it an accident that people who use inventories of aesthetic features pick out such things as boundaries, unity, contrast, and texture. These features are culturally identified as likely to provide enjoyment.

As with art, the aesthetic also depends upon *traditions* in which we share beliefs about what is pleasurable. Valuing some things seems to be a part of most human cultures—sunsets or rhythms, for example. Others are more specific to particular traditions—harmonies enjoyed in the East are not like those enjoyed in the West. And within a society are subcultures that exhibit traditions shared by relatively few people; not everyone appreciates the art of Carl Andre, for instance. When I call you to the window to look at a sunset, I do so knowing that in our culture we share attitudes toward it. Obviously the degree of agreement will not always be so great as it is with sunsets. If I invite you to travel with me to Hartford, Connecticut, to see *Stone Field*, I must believe that we share subcultural traditions that place value on things extolled by the avant-garde. In any case, if delight is *aesthetic*, then there must be something about the object or event to which one can point—color or beat or sleekness—that we agree is what we respond to positively. Even if you and I disagree over whether a song has an interesting harmonic structure, harmony is itself a feature considered aesthetically important in our culture.

Another recurring strain in our history helps us to specify what the proper object of positive *aesthetic* experience is: Aesthetic delight is delight taken in intrinsic features of the object or event. This idea is emphasized in theories of *inherent* aesthetic value. But I believe that 'intrinsic' should be understood as including not just properties that formalists insisted we restrict ourselves to (color, light, or shape) but also things like subject matter, ideas, associations. This way of interpreting 'intrinsic' allows us to include the sort of 'extrinsic' feature that, say, Putnam cherishes—awareness of different ways of viewing the world. The *locus* of attention is the object when our delight is aesthetic, and we recognize that the object is a necessary part of the *cause* of our pleasure. This is why so much emphasis has been put on the role of the object or event in aesthetic experiences. However, these experiences may also involve reflection upon things not strictly inside an object.

Aesthetic experience includes attention to such properties as colors and shapes, but we also think about other things—when and where the artist lived, the way children learn by imitating their parents, the distance of a cathedral from the palace in a medieval city, or a world in which everyone is hateful. One can be interested in or take pleasure in just thinking about these things. The pleasure is aesthetic only when thinking is tied to perception of or reflection upon features in and of the object or event to which we direct our attention. Thus I propose the following definitions:

> Aesthetic experience is experience of instrinsic features of things or events traditionally recognized as worthy of attention and reflection.
>
> Aesthetic value is the value a thing or event has due to its capacity to evoke pleasure that is recognized as arising from features in the object traditionally considered worthy of attention and reflection.

We can identify which intrinsic properties a tradition considers worthy of sustained attention by observing and reflecting upon the vocabularies used to describe objects when people say they are having an aesthetic experience. Our languages and what we value are tightly interwoven. As we learn to use words, we also learn what our culture considers worth talking about. Thus aesthetic values are transmitted through language. In our culture it is considered worthwhile to look at the colors of a sunset, listen to the beat of a song, watch the "rapid twisting of legs," as Tolstoy put it. People also value evidence of an artist's skill and enjoy learning how different individuals think about love or death. When attention is directed to such intrinsic properties, aesthetic experience results; when pleasure is produced from such attention, it is aesthetic pleasure.

We can now answer the question posed at the beginning of Chapter 3: How do we know when and whether someone is having or has had an aesthetic experience? Since this type of experience demands attention to intrinsic properties that a culture deems worthy of such attention, one must know whether the properties are considered worthy and know that a person is attending to them. The former requires knowledge about the culture; the latter typically comes from the language a person uses to describe his or her experience. Someone who says, "Just look at the intricate design of that vase," is undoubtedly having an aesthetic experience.

We can also answer the question posed at the beginning of this chapter about the value of the tulip vase. It has aesthetic value in a culture in which people take delight in intrinsic properties of the vase that are identified as worthy of attention and reflection. The colors, design, shape, and other features that provide evidence of skilled craftsmanship are appreciated. The *amount* of value depends upon the amount of pleasure, which in turn is affected both quantitatively and qualitatively by the properties. The vase probably will not repay as much sustained attention and reflection as will the Van Gogh or Steen paintings we have considered.

Having defined 'aesthetic value', we can deal with practical or "applied" aesthetic questions. If a society believes that it will benefit from a population in which delight results from attention and reflection given to certain intrinsic features, it will attempt to provide opportunities for aesthetic experiences. There may even be reasons to believe that sustained attention and reflection to intrinsic features improves people intellectually and morally. If it does, it will clearly be in the best interest of society to support aesthetic and artistic activities.

Aesthetic experiences are rarely "pure." Descriptions of a person's reactions include references to extrinsic as well as intrinsic properties. The consequences of engaging in aesthetic activity are often as important as the inherent pleasure obtained from them. Moral sensitivity does not rule out aesthetic sensitivity. When my mother described her reaction to *Mother*, she used words such as 'hurtful' as well as 'ugly'. But it is as unreasonable to deny an aesthetic component to her experience because she thought about the feelings of the artist's mother as it would be to deny a moral component because she noticed colors. Moral sensitivity and aesthetic sensitivity are not mutually exclusive; they may be related, as Savile and Putnam suggest.

Suppose that on some March day at what is clearly and depressingly not yet the end of a very bad winter, I happen to see a male cardinal perched on a branch outside my office window. The tree is leafless, the sky gray, the snow dirty. The red is spectacular. I am convinced that anyone who happens to come into my office at that moment will be as delighted as I am by the bird. No special sensitivity is required; no special curriculum would be a prerequisite for the pleasure. All that is needed is shared traditions and a readiness and ability to stop and indulge in the sensation.

We cannot cleanly separate the aesthetic responder in us from our other human concerns. The visitor to my office may be distracted; perhaps he just got back an "F" paper and is unable to enjoy the bird at that moment. I may be visited by someone who hates birds, or red, or the two together. Pornographic depictions of women in bondage being tortured may not (one hopes *will* not) be enjoyable no matter how vivid the colors or well-composed the shapes. Our porcelain tulip vase may so remind us of the abuses of royalty that it may dismay rather than delight us.

If by 'inherent' one means 'separable from all other areas of our experience', then aesthetic value is consequential. If 'consequential' means 'independent of the pleasure or displeasure the object itself gives us', then aesthetic value must be inherent. Both factors, I think, are part of aesthetic experiences. Aesthetic values are subjective to the extent that we are personally involved in aesthetic experiences. Aesthetic value is a result both of the pleasure or displeasure we feel and of our beliefs about what the objects have to offer in other areas of our lives. We do not just perceive; we think about objects, reflecting on their intrinsic properties and on the consequences of such attention and reflection. Aesthetic value is objective to the extent that it depends on particular cultural traditions. Examination of those traditions tells us what individuals within a culture value aesthetically.[27]

| SUMMARY

Aesthetic value can be explained in terms of properties of things valued in and of themselves or in terms of a connection to other sources of value such as goodness or truth. Questions of aesthetic value arise both for individuals and societies. In societies, aesthetic values are related to social values and become issues of public policy. The use of public money to support aesthetic activity or decisions about how to maintain and improve environmental resources demand attention to aesthetic issues. In aesthetic experience, people attend to and reflect upon intrinsic properties that are traditionally deemed worthy of such attention and reflection. Something is aesthetically valuable when attention to and reflection upon such intrinsic properties yields pleasure or contributes positively to other human concerns. Aesthetic value is a matter both of individual responses to things and the social and cultural context of those responses.

The questions that Socrates asked at the beginning of this book are still with us. Several others have been raised along the way. I hope that some readers have been spurred to try to answer some of them.

NOTES

1. Stuart Hampshire, "Logic and Appreciation," in *Aesthetics and Language*, ed. William Elton (Oxford: Basil Blackwell, 1959), p. 166.

2. Monroe Beardsley, *Aesthetics* (New York: Harcourt Brace Jovanovich, 1958).

3. Ibid., p. 531.

4. Leo Tolstoy, *What Is Art?*, trans. Aylmer Maude (London: Oxford University Press, 1930; first published 1898). See especially Chapter 4.

5. Anthony Savile, *The Test of Time* (Oxford: Clarendon Press, 1982), p. 93.

6. Hilary Putnam, "Literature, Science, and Reflection," in *Meaning and the Moral Sciences* (Boston: Routledge & Kegan Paul, 1978), pp. 89–90.

7. Hampshire, "Logic and Appreciation," p. 162.

8. Douglas Morgan, "Does Art Tell the Truth?", *Journal of Aesthetics and Art Criticism* 26 (1967): 17–27.

9. Morris Weitz, "Truth in Literature," *Revue International de Philosophie* 9 (1955): 116–29.

10. Morgan, "Does Art Tell the Truth?", p. 19.

11. I. A. Richards, "Art, Play, and Civilization," in *Principles of Literary Criticism* (New York: Harcourt Brace Jovanovich, Harvest Books, first published 1925), p. 228.

12. Richards, "Badness in Poetry," in *Principles of Literary Criticism*, p. 199.

13. See Richard Smardon, "The Interface of Legal and Esthetic Considerations," in *Proceedings of Our Natural Landscape, A Conference on Applied Techniques for Analysis and Management of the Visual Resources*, General Technical Report PSW-35. (Berkeley, Calif.: U.S. Department of Agriculture, Forest Service, Pacific Southwest Forest and Range Experiment Station, 1979), pp. 676–85.

14. Douglas Stalker and Clark Glymour, "The Malignant Object: Thoughts on Public Sculpture," *Journal of the Public Interest* no. 66 (Winter 1982): 3–21.

15. Ibid., p. 7.

16. Ibid., pp. 14–15.

17. John Beardsley, "Paradigms in Public Sculpture," in *Journal of the Public Interest* no. 66 (Winter 1982): 24–27.

18. David Pole, "Presentational Objects and Their Interpretation," *Philosophy and the Arts*, Royal Institute of Philosophy Lecture Series, 6, 1971–72 (London: Macmillan, 1973), pp. 147–64.

19. Nelson Goodman, *Languages of Art* (Indianapolis: Bobbs-Merrill, 1968).

20. An example of the simplest sort of quantitative study is *National Opinions Concerning the California Desert Conservation Area*. Conducted for the Department of the Interior, Bureau of Land Management, The Gallup Organization, Inc., Princeton, N.J., January 1978. A more sophisticated statistical model is described in Raymond E. Christal, "Selecting a Harem, and Other Applications of the Policy Capturing Model," *Journal of Experimental Education* 36, no. 4 (1968): 35–41.

21. Gabriel J. Cherum and David E. Traweek, "Visitor Employed Photography: A Tool for Interpretive Planning on River Environments," in *Proceedings: River Recreation Management and Research Symposium* (Minneapolis: University of Minnesota, 1977), pp. 83–90.

22. See, for example, David A. King, "Economic Evaluation of Alternative Uses of Rivers," in *Proceedings: River Recreation Management and Research Symposium*.

23. For an example of a psychological study, see Barrie B. Greenbie, "Problems of Scale and Context in Assessing a Generalized Landscape for Particular Persons," in *Landscape Assessment: Values, Perceptions, and Resources*, ed. Ervin H. Zube, Robert O. Brush, and Julius Gy. Fabos (Stroudsberg, Pa: Dowden, Hutchinson & Ross, 1975), pp. 65–91. For examples of motivational studies, see Stephen Kaplan and Rachel Kaplan, eds., *Humanscape: Environments for People* (North Scituate, Mass.: Duxbury Press, 1978).

24. John W. Winton and Geraldine Gender, "Visual Resources of the New Jersey Pine Barrens," in *Proceedings of Our Natural Landscape*, p. 456.

25. R. Burton Litton, Robert J. Tetlow, Jens Sorensen, and Russell A. Beatty, *Water and Landscape* (Port Washington, N.Y.: Water Information Center, 1974).

26. I. C. Laurie, "Aesthetic Factors in Visual Evaluation," in *Landscape Assessment*.

27. For a full discussion of this view, see Marcia M. Eaton, *Aesthetics and the Good Life*, forthcoming.

Index